# CONTENTS

# PREFACE

Carl Becker, some thirty years ago, defined historiography as "that phase of [intellectual history] which records what men have at different times known and believed about the past, the use they have made, in the service of their interests and aspirations, of their knowledge and beliefs, and the underlying presuppositions which have made their knowledge seem to them relevant and their beliefs seem to them true."[*] This book is concerned with what five of the most significant historians of the post-World War II period have known and believed about the past. These brilliant members of their profession have also been the influential spokesmen for a generation whose interests and aspirations were directed toward furthering a liberal democracy.

These men, whose presuppositions were shaped by the continuous threats to liberalism of the last forty years, found that the knowledge and beliefs of their own intellectual fathers, the Progressive historians, seemed no longer true or relevant. By the same token, the relevance and truth of much of what the postwar liberal historians have written have been seriously questioned in the last decade by their own intellectual offspring, myself included.

This study, then, is perhaps simply another painful testi-

[*] Carl L. Becker, "What Is Historiography?" *American Historical Review* 44 (October, 1938): 22.

mony to the generation gap between historians, another suggestion that perhaps the search for the truth about the past is no more than a "noble dream." Nevertheless, the historian, although acutely aware of his own and his colleagues' changing perceptions, must not equate historical relativism with ethical relativism. Some articles of faith, some moral convictions, must remain unchanged and absolute, perhaps even if the historical "facts" do not support them. Skepticism of course has its place in intellectual inquiry; but skepticism as the unwillingness to accept life or existing historical research as it is, is not the same thing as that doubt which does not stimulate but paralyzes man's mind. Especially for those who teach and write history because they believe that it must be the conveyor of humanistic values, and especially for those who believe in the value of the democratic system, an unswerving faith in man's capacity to reason seems perhaps of greatest importance.

Despite his own skepticism, Becker, who was himself an early and eloquent spokesman for postwar liberalism, continued to believe that man, if not perfectly rational, must endeavor to "think well"; upon this belief rested Becker's hope that history had some meaning and that the liberal-democratic ideal might some day be fulfilled. Contemporary liberal historians, however, have denied this faith in man's reason, and this denial has made impossible their own noble dreams of a meaningful history and a better world.

# ACKNOWLEDGMENTS

These acknowledgments, like the book itself, will be brief, but no less sincere for their brevity. To my teachers David Van Tassel, Gene Wise, Carl Ubbelohde, and Morrell Heald, for their kind advice and helpful suggestions, and especially to Bertram Wyatt-Brown, for his encouragement, constructive criticisms, and for the subtitle of the book—many thanks.

And to those for whose mere presence I am grateful—my children, Margaret, Elizabeth, John, and Sarah—much love.

The Terrors of Ideological Politics

# CHAPTER 1

## *"LIBERALS OF A VERY CONSERVATIVE AND DISILLUSIONED KIND"*

In 1959 the political theorist Bernard Crick remarked upon the inadequacy for the contemporary period of James Bryce's nineteenth-century analysis of the American political system. Bryce's failing, Crick thought, lay in his "skepticism about the effects of general ideas, such as democracy, upon history which we now, amid the terrors of ideological politics . . . cannot share."[1] Americans had seen abundant evidence of the ability of powerful idea systems, embodied in extremist political movements, to change the course of history. The fascism of Mussolini's Italy and Hitler's Germany had brought in its wake the brutal suppression of civil and political liberties, the cynical persecution and extermination of helpless segments of the population, and nakedly aggressive territorial expansion which culminated in the violence of World War II. Cold War Communism, rising out of the ashes of the fascist defeat and relying upon political and military terrorism, threatened nuclear holocaust in its drive for power. Both dynamic creeds endangered democracy. But, as Crick suggested, by the late 1950's democracy had, for some, become identified with just this kind of terrifying totalitarian political philosophy.

This metamorphosis of the traditional American faith in democracy is illustrated in the work of five of the most prominent historians of the post-World War II era: Arthur M. Schlesinger, Jr., Louis Hartz, Daniel J. Boorstin, Edmund S.

3

Morgan, and Richard Hofstadter. These historians have held forth at the most prestigious American universities— Harvard, Yale, Columbia, and the University of Chicago— and their influence upon their colleagues as well as upon their students is unquestionable. Their written history broke new historiographical ground in the 1940's, dominated the thinking of the historical guild during the next decade, and has only recently been challenged. Their distrust of ideology has been noted by both their apologists and their critics, who have maintained that it reflected simply the prosperity of the Eisenhower years, the anxieties of the Cold War, and especially the frightening populistic uprising of McCarthyism. Valid proof of these contentions is the patently conservative cast of these historians' work during and after the 1950's: their emphasis on the unanimity of American political thought, on the stability of American political and social institutions, and on the uniqueness of American experience. Accordingly, these men have been christened "consensus" historians, "counter-Progressives," or "neo-conservatives."[2]

Yet at the risk of straining the already overloaded vocabulary of American historiography, it would be more appropriate to call them "liberal" historians, for their principal concern has been liberalism and the intellectual whom they see as its vehicle.[3] Their liberalism has been a product of the painful reassessment of the American reform tradition which began in the 1930's. In this reappraisal the distrust of ideology has consistently played a significant role, and the common concern of these historians has been to divest liberalism and the intellectual of ideology.

In reaction to the rigidities of the Marxism prevalent in the intellectual community during the 1930's, ideology was identified by liberals with an unchanging idea system or an absolute, incongruent with present realities.[4] Yet the American reform tradition to which these men turned also contained ideological elements. Nineteenth-century liberals in the tradition of Jefferson and Jackson had left a heritage of economic individualism which fostered laissez-faire government and capitalism; the disaster of the Great Depression made free enterprise seem absurdly unrealistic. The Progressive reformers of the twentieth century, critical—although not critical enough—of free enterprise, inherited from the Enlightenment and the Romanticism of the earlier period the belief that man, inherently possessed of both reason and moral sense, was perfectible and hence capable of self-government; to the new historians this sanguine view of man appeared untenable in the face of the political behavior of the followers of Hitler, Mussolini, and Stalin. Moreover, this faith in man had prevented Progressives from achieving significant economic reforms, as evidenced by the persistence of capitalism in the depths of a depression. As initially conceived, therefore, the ideologies of capitalism and man's perfectibility made Progressivism too conservative for the tastes of those who came of age in the 1930's. Yet these men also realized that the liberal faith in reason and morality, particularly as this was embodied in the intellectual, provided reform with its driving impulse. However, when Joseph McCarthy perverted this concept of the intellectual and turned the weapons of reform upon the intellectual community itself, ideological politics became terrifying, political democracy became a frightening phenomenon, and American liberalism became identified with the capitalism the liberals had earlier rejected.

The liberal historians were born between 1914 and 1917 and reached intellectual maturity during the chaotic Depression decade when, as young college and graduate students, they were made aware of the political force of ideologies. As Hofstadter explained, "I belong to a generation which came of age during . . . a period . . . of tremendous conflict on a world scale and of intense and lively controversy in American domestic politics. A battle of ideologies roughly similar to that which took place in a world-wide theatre of action could be seen at home as well."[5] His contemporary and colleague Alfred Kazin echoed Hofstadter's judgment of the period: "It was as if the planet had locked in combat—unrest and unemployment, the political struggles inside the New Deal, suddenly became part of the single pattern of struggle against Franco and his allies Hitler and Mussolini."[6]

In response to this "single pattern" of ideological politics on the right, the American intellectuals moved to the left, for Marxism seemed to promise the solution to current ills. Few intellectuals were orthodox or doctrinaire Marxists; fewer still were members of the Communist party. Kazin, for example, also spoke of the varieties of leftism espoused by his peers: "Socialists who were Norman Thomas Socialists, old-line Social Democrats, Austro-Marxists; [and] Communists who were Stalinist centrists, Trotskyite leftists, Lovestoneite right-wingers, Musteites and Fieldites."[7] All, however, shared a common fear of the fascism which thrived on the poverty and bruised national egos of Italy and Germany left in the wake of the Treaty of Versailles. Hitler and Mussolini made a mockery of the political process by overthrowing legitimate republican governments and crushing political opposition and a sham of the League of Nations by their seizures of Ethiopia, Austria, and Czechoslovakia. The fascist support of Franco's regime in the Spanish Civil War aroused the sympathies of the American intellectual community for the Loyalist forces aided by the Soviet Union. Russia seemed the last bulwark against the Axis.

This country seemed ripe for fascism as well. In 1935 Sinclair Lewis attempted to persuade those who believed it couldn't "happen here" that fascism was a potential reality. Capitalism, long under fire by the intelligentsia for fostering both materialism and a disparity of wealth, had seemingly collapsed. Millions were without jobs; angry farmers and workers rioted and struck, while the urban middle class shamefacedly stood in bread lines or applied for relief, and those who still had money worried nervously about the unrest stirred up by "Reds" and Socialists. As Roosevelt and the Congress fumbled for the solutions to poverty and unemployment, extremists on the right—from Father Coughlin and Huey Long to homegrown fascists like William Dudley Pelley's Silver Shirts—challenged the democratic process and proposed their own panaceas. The failure of free enterprise threatened to bring political democracy toppling down with it; unregulated capitalism was clearly inoperable, and to intellectuals, already accustomed to think in terms of social planning, some form of socialism seemed the answer.

The intellectuals' brief flirtation with the Marxist left reached its climax in 1935 with the Popular Front, the Communist effort to identify itself with American reform in order to enlist United States aid for the Soviet Union, imperiled by the increasingly aggressive fascist powers. However, the shifts in Communist foreign policy had already bewildered some American leftists, while the Moscow trials in 1936 and the subsequent party purges alienated others. When the Soviet Union and Germany signed the nonaggression pact of 1939 and Russia invaded Finland, it became painfully apparent to American intellectuals that Communism was no less totalitarian than fascism; Soviet Marxism did not square with the democratic realities of American life and was, therefore, ideological.

Disenchanted not with radicalism but with the party line, the college generation of the thirties turned to the American past to find justification for their own reformism. The version of the past to which they turned was that of the Progressive historians—Charles A. Beard, Carl L. Becker, Vernon L. Parrington, Frederick Jackson Turner, and their disciples.[8] These men, Hofstadter later said, "explained the American liberal mind to itself in historical terms."[9] Progressive historiography was shaped by the reformist impulses of the early twentieth century which took political form in the presidencies of Theodore Roosevelt and Woodrow Wilson. Its revival in the thirties was due perhaps to the fact that it shared some significant perspectives with discredited Marxism: its criticism of laissez-faire, its emphasis on economic and class conflict, and its concern for the common man. Progressive historians described the American past from the Revolution onward as a continuous struggle between economic interest groups—merchants versus farmers, rich versus poor, East versus West, debtors versus creditors. This conflict was headed ultimately and inevitably toward the Progressive goal of a more genuinely participatory democracy, a goal based, first, on the belief that man as a rational, moral being was capable of self-government, and second, on the idea that economic equality was a precondition for equal political participation. These reformers, therefore, advocated government regulation of the economy in order to achieve economic justice. The Progressive tradition offered a corrective to free enterprise and strengthened the faltering faith in democracy.

The Progressive historians also explained why Americans bitterly resisted even the mild attempts made by Roosevelt to impose some restrictions upon capitalism, for according to Progressive thought, man's tendency to cling to obsolete notions about free enterprise was rooted in his self-interestedness. Progressives attacked such outmoded ideas with the pragmatic epistemology they had inherited from the reformers of the Gilded Age, who had attempted to combat the late nineteenth-century version of economic individualism, Spencerian Social Darwinism. Pragmatism lent itself to reform because its central postulate held that the truth of an idea is not defined by an abstract moral absolute but by man's own ever-changing experience. Pragmatism was also congenial to the younger generation of liberals because it avoided the rigid, doctrinaire quality of Marxist thought. With pragmatism as a basis, the Progressives argued, as had their predecessors, that man's institutions—particularly his government—must change, like truth itself, in order to serve his present needs better.

The pragmatic epistemology was a useful weapon in the battle for reform, as was its logical corollary, historical relativism. Beard and Becker, the leading American exponents of historical relativism, maintained that history's function was to deal with contemporary problems and present solutions to them by weaning man away from those ideas and values and institutions which were outdated.[10] The Progressives conceived of the historian in their own image: as the reformist intellectual, who, like themselves, examined the past with an eye to needed change in the present. In their scheme, the intellectual could transcend his immediate experience by virtue of his reason; it was he who provided the unchanging ideals and moral values for the future, uninfluenced by self-interest or his material environment. In this role, he also rescued Progressive thought from the materialism and determinism implicit in its economic emphasis and the ethical relativism inherent in the pragmatic concept of truth.[11]

Thus, the liberal historians began their professional careers in the early 1940's, inspired by the Progressive goal of political democracy and economic justice, and armed with pragmatism to challenge the ideology of free enterprise. The function of the intellectual, as they conceived it, would be to counter self-interest with moral values, thereby bringing about the desired change in the economic and political status quo.

Yet this was Progressivism with a difference, for European totalitarianism had exposed a serious Progressive failing— the optimistic belief in man's rationality and perfectibility. To a generation that had witnessed racist pogroms and murders, nationalistic war and aggression, and a lust for political power which swept constitutional liberties before it, Progressive liberalism seemed hopelessly naïve. This naïveté had led to the Progressive reliance on ineffectual political devices like the initiative and referendum which left capitalism untouched, and, more important, had left intellectuals vulnerable to Soviet Marxism and disillusion in the thirties. The faith in man's perfectibility did not square with the obvious fact of his imperfection; this "perfectionism" was, therefore, ideological.

The need for a more "realistic" version of liberalism was obvious. As Schlesinger recounted,

> Official liberalism has long been almost inextricably linked with a picture of man as perfectible, as endowed with sufficient wisdom and selflessness to endure power and to use it infallibly for the general good. The Soviet experience, on top of the rise of fascism, reminded my generation rather forcibly that man was indeed imperfect.[12]

Rejecting what they considered the "too abstract, too ambitious and too crude ideas" of their elders, these young men became "liberals of a very conservative and disillusioned kind"[13] in the name of more radical reform.

They found confirmation for their suspicions of Progressivism in a second group of thinkers with a common interest in dynamic idea systems with noneconomic origins: Reinhold Niebuhr, Erich Fromm, Alexis de Tocqueville, Max Weber, and Karl Mannheim.[14] These social scientists explained the power of both the totalitarian creeds and Progressivism itself in terms of an analysis of human nature more congruent with the realities as young liberals saw them. Niebuhr and Fromm concluded that the appeal of totalitarianism lay in man's irrationality and sense of inadequacy. The theologian Niebuhr maintained that because man is tainted by original sin his reason is impaired, but because man also has free will he is continually driven to escape the finiteness of his own mind and to seek God-like perfection. He is, therefore, attracted to those political philosophies which stress his goodness, his rationality, and his power to control history. Fromm, examining the problem as a social psychologist, reached similar conclusions: man's feelings of isolation and anxiety, heightened by his ability to reason, lead him to "escape from freedom" into the security of an all-encompassing political faith which promises him something more than his imperfect humanity. Tocqueville, the astute commentator on Jacksonian democracy, found that its social and political equality fostered in man both a craving for perfecting himself and his institutions and a fear of his own insignificance that led him to succumb to the tyranny of the majority. Both totalitarianism and Progressive liberalism, therefore, drew their strength from their promise that man could perfect himself and his society,[15] and both harbored the seeds of political despotism and authoritarianism.

The social scientists, however, like the Progressives, were pragmatists, for they too distrusted absolutes. Believing that truth was determined by man's immediate and changing experience, they too struggled with the problems of determinism and ethical relativism. And, like the Progressives, the social scientists, particularly Weber and Mannheim, argued that the intellectual or the man of reason was unhampered by his temporal and material environment in his search for truth. Although peculiarly susceptible to perfectionist political philosophies, the intellectual was also the vehicle for change and the formulator of ideals; it was the man of reason who transformed political and economic conflicts into moral struggles.

These younger historians, therefore, built their own version of liberalism upon these two sometimes contradictory analyses of ideology. Liberalism must rid itself of the ideology of economic individualism and capitalism, so ill adapted to the economic realities of the Depression, and rid itself as well of the belief in man's perfectibility, so incompatible with the realities of European totalitarianism. Further, liberalism must somehow combine the Progressive ideal of political democracy with the realistic picture of man provided by the social scientist; it must retain both the Progressive economic interpretation and the dynamic analysis of ideas furnished by the social scientists. The responsibility for maintaining this tenuous equilibrium of idealism and realism lay with the intellectual. It fell to him to provide those unchanging moral values which would counter the ideology of capitalism and effect reform; at the same time, however, he must not succumb to the ideology of perfectionism which led to Marxism and disenchantment or to the ineffectual reformism of the Progressives.

This balance was all the more difficult to achieve since the definition of ideology as incongruent with present reality made it necessary for liberalism to adapt constantly to changing historical situations. Each shift in external circumstances was to be reflected in the twists and turns of liberal thought during the next three decades, and each twist and turn would mean a discarding not only of Progressive assumptions but of the younger liberals' own positions. One price of a nonideological liberalism has been the tortuous nature of its intellectual development as liberals recanted and repented of their own sins until they were forced by the pressure of circumstances to admit the logic of their own initial premises.

The difficulty of adapting to meet the challenges of ideology is illustrated in the first books of the liberal historians, published from the early to mid-forties, which revealed the impact of the American entrance into World War II upon the liberal community. The younger generation approved of United States involvement in the war against the Axis but was simultaneously critical of the increasing conservatism of wartime domestic politics. Liberals in the Progressive tradition, however, remembering the disastrous aftermath of the First World War, which had made the world not safe for democracy but ripe for totalitarianism, and persuaded by the Nye Committee's findings on the selfish economic motivations behind our entrance into that war, were slow to respond to Roosevelt's efforts at collective security until after Hitler had taken most of western Europe, and France had fallen in 1940. The doubts of these liberals about the wisdom of American involvement ended after Pearl Harbor, although the intractable Beard, still active in the forties, argued that Roosevelt had manipulated the Japanese into attacking to provide him with a pretext for declaring war. In this context, Morgan, writing in 1942 and 1943 of the "tribalism" of the Puritans, who forfeited their opportunity to save the world by concentrating on saving themselves and their children,[16] also chided his fellow liberals for refusing to recognize their responsibilities; when Morgan maintained that the Puritan way of life and thought collapsed because the Puritans failed to face the fact of man's inherent inadequacies, the reference to those isolationists who refused to understand the dangers of totalitarianism was implicit.

As United States aid to the embattled Allies increased, "Dr. New Deal" gave way to "Dr. Win the War." The Depression was beaten, not by reform measures but by the prosperity of wartime industries. The energies of the Roosevelt administration were concentrated on utilizing free enterprise to win the war rather than, as the young liberals had hoped, on doing away with it. Capitalism was given a new lease on life; the ideology of laissez-faire was revitalized. Thus, Hofstadter's *Social Darwinism in American Thought* (1944), Hartz' *Economic Policy and Democratic Thought* (1948), and Boorstin's *Mysterious Science of the Law* (1941) hammered home the conservatism inherent in the liberal ideology of economic individualism. All three books also contrasted the effectiveness of pragmatism with the futility of systematic or rationalized systems of thought in order to criticize the Progressive programmatic solutions to economic maladjustment—the New Nationalism and the New Freedom used ineffectively by Roosevelt. The pragmatic stress on ends over means also justified the renewed American friendship with the Soviet Union, scorned and distrusted by liberals after the Nazi-Soviet Pact but now an ally sorely needed in the battle against the Axis.

Schlesinger's *The Age of Jackson* (1945) provided the best summary of liberal thinking during this period. The thesis of the book was that a political democracy could be based only upon an equitable distribution of wealth achieved through government regulation, but that the necessary reforms must rest also upon a realistic assessment of man's capabilities. Schlesinger's analysis of the desirable role of the intellectual reinforced this message. He contrasted those ineffectual intellectuals who dreamed of perfection without involvement in sordid reality with pragmatic politicians who approached reform through economics. The realists ultimately triumphed, but the utopian intellectuals provided reform with moral direction and with the ideals necessary to offset materialism and relativism.

By 1948, however, the international situation of this country had changed again. First, the honeymoon with the Soviet Union—the conferences at Teheran and Yalta and the co-operative efforts to found the United Nations—was over. As Stalin broke wartime agreements and Russian delegates sabotaged the early sessions of the UN, Truman retaliated with the Truman Doctrine and the Marshall Plan, providing aid to anti-Communist regimes. The Cold War had begun, and the United States found itself facing another and more powerful totalitarian ideology.

Second, Roosevelt's death in 1945 had left domestic liberalism a shambles. Liberal hopes had been raised high by his proclamation of an Economic Bill of Rights, promising a resurgence of the New Deal reform thrust on an international level at the war's end. Truman, however, did not move in the direction of further regulation of free enterprise but vacillated on issues like wage and price controls, and the Republican Eightieth Congress struck vigorously at New Deal measures. Moreover, the liberal coalition had been held together in large part by Roosevelt's personal charm. With this gone, the Democratic party splintered in the 1948 presidential campaign: Truman retained the support of the greatest portion of party membership, which won him his narrow victory, but Henry Wallace and Strom Thurmond led off the left and right wings of the party. Wallace's Progressive party capitalized upon both the increasingly conservative tenor of economic policy and Truman's belligerency toward the Soviet Union; the Progressive platform called for the nationalization of basic industries and a softer stand toward Russia, both positions similar to those taken by liberals in the early forties. Communist infiltration of this party led by the former New Dealer, however, aroused liberal fears that they themselves were still, as in the 1930's, susceptible to this brand of perfectionism.

Much of the blame for liberal political sins could, it seemed, be placed upon the earlier enthusiastic support of Progressive pragmatism. The folly of allowing, in pragmatic fashion, the end of winning the war to justify the means—the alliance with Russia and the revival of capitalism—was now obvious. Moreover, the pragmatic method too readily assumed that man was rational enough to find truth without fixed philosophical guidelines, and this overoptimistic assumption had left liberalism still vulnerable to the renewed challenges of capitalism and perfectionism.

Accordingly, the liberal historians in the late forties and early fifties rejected pragmatism and pointed to the need for clearly defined and articulated philosophical and moral underpinnings for the liberal position. Both Hofstadter in *The American Political Tradition* (1948) and Hartz in *The Liberal Tradition in America* (1955) accused the Progressives and the New Dealers of unconsciously entertaining obsolete idea systems which prevented genuine economic reform. For Hofstadter, liberalism was hampered by its ties to the Protestant ethic, whose implicit support of capitalism and stress on man's moral nature were both unrealistic. For Hartz, the liberal tradition was simply an irrational manifestation of John Locke's seventeenth-century philosophy, in which the emphasis on private property sanctioned laissez-faire and the concept of the right of revolution supported the Progressives' utopian notion that man could change and better his society.

These books indicate that the struggle for political democracy both at home and abroad was construed less in terms of conflict between economic interests than between opposing philosophies, a conflict in which liberalism was weakened by being unaware of its own assumptions. Hence, both Hofstadter and Hartz insisted that liberalism, in self-defense, must rest upon firmer intellectual and moral grounds. Boorstin's *The Lost World of Thomas Jefferson* (1948) bore the same message. Contemporary liberal thought, Boorstin said, had not relinquished Jeffersonian naturalism;

the moral relativism inherent in naturalism left liberals susceptible to European perfectionism and domestic capitalism. Again, Schlesinger made most explicit the assumptions and difficulties of liberalism in this period. In *The Vital Center* (1949) he called for the formulation of a coherent, principled, but realistic liberalism to combat the forces of big business at home and Communism abroad and within liberal ranks. Yet although it should have been the function of the intellectual to define such a philosophy or to clarify unconscious or irrational liberal premises, Schlesinger was increasingly distrustful of the intellectual, whose perfectionist tendencies had led him to desert the New Deal for Wallace.

Subsequent events, however, made this plea for a morally and intellectually consistent liberalism seem both irrelevant and dangerous. Truman's upset victory over the Republican Dewey and the Progressive Wallace temporarily laid to rest liberal fears of a resurgent capitalism or perfectionism. Truman's Fair Deal promised a revival of reformism, and his loyalty program in 1947 designed to weed Communists out of the federal government indicated liberal awareness of the danger of Communism. The policy of containment, relying heavily on economic aid as in the Marshall Plan, was formulated to combat Communist successes in China and the lowering of the iron curtain over the Russian satellites. The establishment of the North Atlantic Treaty Organization and American intervention in Korea in 1950 indicated that this country was not going to revert to its prewar isolationism. Eisenhower's election in 1952 only temporarily threatened to reverse these heartening trends. In spite of his own personal preference for free enterprise, Eisenhower, who had been considered presidential timber by the liberal wing of the Democratic party in 1948, maintained the substance of the New Deal intact. The prosperity of the early fifties made welfare capitalism more palatable to liberals.

Secretary of State John Foster Dulles attempted to substitute brinkmanship for containment, but the substitution was more rhetorical than real.

In this context, the development of a clearly defined liberal philosophy would only destroy the new comity between Republicans and Democrats, just as the formulation of a democratic counterphilosophy would increase the dangers of a global conflict between the United States and the Soviet Union. Liberalism had apparently triumphed over ideology with the general acceptance of some measure of economic regulation and of anti-Communist internationalism.

Yet it was a hollow victory, for liberalism was increasingly threatened by Joseph McCarthy, whose brand of ideological politics challenged the realities of the New Deal welfare state and the policy of containment in such a way that the last ties between liberalism and its Progressive heritage—the belief in political democracy and in the intellectual as reformer—were snapped. The Senator from Wisconsin represented a vicious parody of the Progressive ideal. He was himself a kind of latter-day Progressive, occupying the Senate seat of the son of the great Progressive leader Robert LaFollette. His attacks on containment were reminiscent of the Midwestern Progressive isolationism of LaFollette and Beard. McCarthy appeared to have a mass popular following and to have aroused the kind of participatory democracy which the Progressives had hoped for.[17] In addition, the bulk of this following was drawn from a middle class salvaged from the Depression by New Deal measures designed to foster a more equitable distribution of wealth, the Progressive means to their end. But the results were hardly what the Progressives had envisioned, for from the liberal perspective, McCarthyism bore all the earmarks of European totalitarianism: the suppression of dissent and the curtailment of civil liberties, character assassinations, demagogic appeals and illicit use of political power, and the humbling of two Presidents and the United States Congress.[18] McCarthyism, in short, confirmed liberal suspicions, planted by the realistic social scientists, that Progressive perfectionism harbored totalitarianism, and McCarthy's anti-Communism reawakened liberal fears of native fascism.

But if the Progressives had been wrong about the virtues of democratic man, McCarthyism also made it obvious that the liberals themselves had misconstrued their own role as intellectuals, a role assigned to them by the Progressives. For the Senator was also a frightening perversion of their own concept of the man of reason as a vehicle for change and the moral counterforce to ideology. Playing upon Cold War anxieties about Communism, heightened and confirmed by the liberals themselves and by Truman's loyalty program in the late forties, McCarthy attacked the New Deal welfare state as Communist-inspired. He also usurped the liberal plea that the conflict between Communism and democracy be fought on moral grounds and insisted, as liberals themselves had, that the philosophical lines between the two could and must be clearly drawn. Capitalizing upon the fact of liberal leftism in the Depression years and upon the liberals' own distrust of the intellectual for his perfectionist tendencies, McCarthy ruthlessly charged the intellectual community with subversion and fellow-traveling, echoing their own self-accusations. The resulting wave of popular anti-intellectualism, testified to by the defeat of Adlai Stevenson in 1952, persuaded the liberal historians that they themselves had not been sufficiently realistic. Having miscast themselves as champions of political democracy and economic equality, they had unwittingly but deservedly aroused the wrath of an ungrateful and irrational people. The totalitarian impulse inherent in political democracy was, therefore, fostered by the perfectionist intellectual himself, who attempted to equate that democracy with conflict over moral issues.

The impact of McCarthyism is revealed by these historians' third books. Although still present, the ideology of capitalism did not play the important role here. Of much greater significance was the ideological belief in perfectionism, now identified explicitly with European totalitarianism and implicitly with the liberal intellectual. In *The Age of Reform* (1955) Hofstadter argued that neither Populism nor Progressivism had led to needed economic reforms, because they sought a reversion to laissez-faire. More important, Hofstadter suggested that the Progressive intellectuals' unrealistic notion of man and their stress on moralism encouraged the participatory democracy evident in McCarthyism. Morgan's *Stamp Act Crisis* (1953) implied that the introduction of moral absolutes into politics by the intellectual leaders of the American Revolution caused the rise of political demagogues and the destruction of political reputations. Boorstin maintained in *The Genius of American Politics* (1953) that the moderation and conservatism of American political thought stemmed from its traditional disregard of moral issues, and he warned American intellectuals against formulating political philosophies, which he now equated with European totalitarianism.

By destroying the intellectual's faith in himself, McCarthyism destroyed the precarious liberal balance between realism and idealism: in subsequent works, realism triumphed. Liberalism became identified with economic self-interest rather than morality, and democracy became synonymous with capitalism. The reforming intellectual became the architect of the status quo.

The Progressive version of the past as a continuous conflict moving toward political democracy was likewise scrapped, and a stress on American consensus, stability, and uniqueness became the trademark of liberal historiography. Schlesinger's "vital center" attempted to establish an inner consensus for liberalism. Hartz searched for that unique identity for the American liberal which would protect him from European ideologies. Boorstin's "community" was directed toward maintaining social and political stability. Morgan defined that "principle" which would make the intellectual invulnerable to perfectionism, while Hofstadter illustrated what that principle would mean in practice.

The keystone of this liberal interpretation of the past lay in its continued insistence upon the nonideological character of liberalism. Yet the intellectual tensions within a nonideological liberalism which rests upon a fear of ideology are obvious, and the attempts to escape the terrors of ideological politics have been logically self-defeating.

## NOTES

1. *The American Science of Politics: Its Origins and Conditions* (Berkeley and Los Angeles: University of California Press, 1959), p. 116.

2. John Higham christened them "consensus" historians in "The Cult of the American Consensus: Homogenizing American History," *Commentary* 27 (February, 1959): 93–100; see also Higham, "Beyond Consensus: The Historian as Moral Critic," *American Historical Review* 67 (April, 1962): 609–25, or Higham et al., *History* (Englewood Cliffs, N.J.: Prentice-Hall, 1965), pp. 212–32. Other discussions of these men as consensus historians are J. Rogers Hollingsworth, "Consensus and Continuity in Recent American Historical Writing," *South Atlantic Quarterly* 61 (Winter, 1962): 40–50; Richard Hofstadter, *The Progressive Historians: Turner, Beard, and Parrington* (New York: Alfred A. Knopf, 1968), pp. 437–66; and J. R. Pole, "The American Past: Is It Still Usable?," *Journal of American Studies* 1 (April, 1967): 63–78. The term "counter-Progressive" is used by Gene Wise, *Explanation in Historical Studies: Some Strategies for Inquiry* (Homewood, Ill.: Dorsey Press, forthcoming). The historians of the New Left stress the inherently conservative nature of liberalism, as in the following: Jesse Lemisch, "The American Revolution Seen from the Bottom Up," in *Towards a New Past: Dissenting Essays in American History*, ed. Barton J. Bernstein (New York: Pantheon Books, 1968); Christopher Lasch, "The Cultural Cold War: A Short History of the Congress for Cultural Freedom," in *Towards a New Past*; Kenneth McNaught, "American Progressivism and the Great Society," *Journal of American History* 53 (December, 1966): 504–20; Norman Pollack, "Fear of Man: Populism, Authoritarianism, and the Historian," *Agricultural History* 39 (April, 1965): 59–76; Warren Susman, "History and the American Intellectual: Uses of a Usable Past," *American Quarterly* 16 (Summer, 1964):

243–63; and Dennis Wrong, "Reflections on the End of Ideology," *Dissent* 7 (Summer, 1960): 286–92.

3.  Marcus Cunliffe makes this observation of Schlesinger in "Arthur M. Schlesinger, Jr.," in *Pastmasters: Some Essays on American Historians*, ed. Marcus Cunliffe and Robin W. Winks (New York: Harper and Row, 1969), pp. 356, 358.

4.  John P. Diggins, "Consciousness and Ideology in American History: The Burden of Daniel J. Boorstin," *American Historical Review* 76 (February, 1971): 110. This is also Karl Mannheim's definition of ideology.

5.  Richard Hofstadter, "History and the Social Sciences," in *The Varieties of History from Voltaire to the Present*, ed. Fritz Stern (New York: Meridian Books, 1959), p. 361.

6.  *Starting Out in the Thirties* (Boston: Little, Brown and Co., 1965), p. 83. Schlesinger, in his essay on Hofstadter in *Pastmasters*, p. 280, notes that Kazin's book mentions Hofstadter under a pseudonym.

7.  *Starting Out in the Thirties*, p. 5. See also Daniel Aaron, *Writers on the Left: Episodes in Literary Communism* (New York: Harcourt, Brace and World, 1961), or Frank A. Warren III, *Liberals and Communism: The "Red Decade" Revisited* (Bloomington and London: Indiana University Press, 1966).

8.  The best source on the Progressive historians is Hofstadter, *The Progressive Historians*; see also Higham, *History*, pp. 171–82.

9.  *The Progressive Historians*, p. xii.

10.  On historical relativism, see Higham, *History*, p. 104–31.

11.  The role of the intellectual is crucial for understanding Progressive thinking. It explains why, despite their typically pragmatic emphasis on the experiential basis of knowledge, Progressives described ideas which fostered change and reform as uninfluenced by the immediate environment or self-interest and those ideas which hindered progress as having material origins, as noted by Robert

Allen Skotheim, *American Intellectual Histories and Historians* (Princeton: Princeton University Press, 1966). Hofstadter also pointed out in *The Progressive Historians*, p. 402, that Parrington's reformers or "liberals" are described as both intellectuals and idealists.

12. Arthur M. Schlesinger, Jr., *The Vital Center: The Politics of Freedom* (Boston: Houghton Mifflin Co., 1949), p. ix.

13. The phrase comes from Richard Chase, *Democratic Vista: A Dialogue on Life and Letters in Contemporary America* (Garden City, N.Y.: Doubleday and Co., 1958), p. 179, where he reconstructs an imaginary dialogue between one of the college generation of the thirties and an older man whose politics resemble those of the Progressives.

14. For an analysis of theological "neo-orthodoxy," of which Niebuhr is the leading American exponent, see William Lee Miller, "The Rise of Theological Orthodoxy," in *Paths of American Thought*, ed. Arthur M. Schlesinger, Jr., and Morton White (Boston: Houghton Mifflin Co., 1963), esp. pp. 327–55. The relationship between Niebuhr and the postwar analysis of foreign policy is described by William T. Bluhm, *Theories of the Political System: Classics of Political Thought and Modern Political Analysis* (Englewood Cliffs, N.J.: Prentice-Hall, 1965), pp. 177–87. Gene Wise has also found evidence of Niebuhr's influence on contemporary historians in "Perry Miller's *New England Mind,*" *Journal of the History of Ideas* 29 (October–December, 1968): 579–600. For background on Fromm and an assessment of his contribution to intellectual history, see Thomas L. Hartshorne, *The Distorted Image: Changing Conceptions of the American Character Since Turner* (Cleveland: The Press of Case Western Reserve University, 1968), pp. 123–36; an excellent critique of Fromm's thought is John H. Schaar, *Escape from Authority: The Perspectives of Erich Fromm* (New York: Basic Books, 1961). The literature on Tocqueville is exten-

sive, but a good recent analysis is Marvin Zetterbaum, *Tocqueville and the Problem of Democracy* (Stanford: Stanford University Press, 1967). H. Stuart Hughes describes the thought of Weber and Mannheim as a reaction to sociological positivism, exemplified by Marx, and links them with American pragmatism in *Consciousness and Society: The Reorientation of European Social Thought, 1890–1930* (New York: Alfred A. Knopf, 1958), pp. 30 ff.

15. Niebuhr makes the analogy between liberalism and Communism in *Reinhold Niebuhr on Politics: His Political Philosophy and Its Application to Our Age as Expressed in His Writings*, ed. Harry R. Davis and Robert C. Good (New York: Charles Scribner's Sons, 1960), pp. 13–40.

16. Edmund Morgan, "The Puritan Family and the Social Order," *More Books*, 6th ser. 38 (January, 1943): 9–21, and "Puritan Tribalism," ibid., pp. 203–19, later published as chapters in *The Puritan Family: Religion and Domestic Relations in Seventeenth-Century New England* (Boston: Public Library, 1944).

17. The thesis of Michael Paul Rogin's *The Intellectuals and McCarthy: The Radical Specter* (Cambridge, Mass., and London: M.I.T. Press, 1967), is that McCarthyism was not in fact a mass movement. However that may be, the significant thing is that McCarthy appeared to these liberals to rally widespread popular support.

18. A good example of the liberal reaction to McCarthy, although it is tempered by time, is Richard Rovere, *Senator Joe McCarthy* (Cleveland and New York: World Publishing Co., 1965).

# CHAPTER 2

# ARTHUR M. SCHLESINGER, JR., AND THE SEARCH FOR THE VITAL CENTER

As the outspoken apologist for postwar liberalism, Arthur M. Schlesinger, Jr., has found historical justification for its practice in *The Age of Jackson*, set forth its theory in *The Vital Center*, and written eloquently of its heroes in *The Age of Roosevelt* and *A Thousand Days*. Some of Schlesinger's critics, noting his animosity toward the business class, have described him as the last of the Progressive historians; others have classified him as an early exponent of postwar conservatism.[1] Schlesinger is difficult to categorize, however, because he illustrates, perhaps more clearly than his liberal colleagues, the ambiguities of a liberalism drawn from both the Progressive idealists and the realistic social scientists. His concept of the "vital center" is intended to achieve the desired balance of idealism and realism which would make the liberal immune to the ideological politics of capitalism and perfectionism.

Progressivism itself had been altered by the events of the 1930's and 1940's, but altered in ways that made it seem more irrelevant to the young liberals. Beard and Becker were still publishing, and although they did not agree on all issues, they were representative of the liberal reaction to the rise of totalitarianism, the Depression, and the entrance of the United States into World War II.

Although not insular, Progressives had always tended to stress the distinctiveness of American experience and to discount its historical and intellectual ties with Europe. This was partly in reaction to their own intellectual predecessors, the scientific evolutionists of the Herbert Baxter Adams school, who had found the origins of American institutions in Europe, and partly in reaction to the disillusioning after-effects of American involvement in World War I. As a result, Progressives had been less drawn to Soviet Marxism during the thirties than were their young liberal disciples. Feeling that their own brand of reform was preferable to a system like Communism which sacrificed political liberties for economic reform, Progressives clung to their hope that their goal of political democracy could be achieved through more moderate American methods.[2]

Beard's resistance to the drift of American foreign policy in the late thirties stemmed from his desire to see this democracy accomplished. Reflecting the isolationist mood of the general public and the strong pacifist movement of the period, Beard supported the Neutrality Acts and opposed Roosevelt's attempts to aid the Allies through Lend-Lease. Although he backed the war effort after Pearl Harbor, at the war's conclusion he destroyed his professional reputation by accusing Roosevelt of engineering the Japanese attack in order to bring this country into the war. Beard's stance was construed by the younger generation as evidence of the shortsightedness and utopianism of Progressive thought, which failed to take seriously the threat of fascism.

The emergence of the powerful fascist and Communist creeds, however, had not in fact left Progressives unscathed. In partial rejection of his early economic interpretation of history, Beard by 1942 admitted "the power of ideas as world views"; "great world views, when imbedded in the convictions of powerful personalities and classes, and tenaciously held by a large portion of the people in general," he said, "exert a tremendous influence on history."[3] However, when

Beard attempted to explain history in terms of ideas, as in *The American Spirit*, his analysis lost that economic realism which liberals had earlier admired. Beard also moved away from pragmatism in reaction to totalitarianism, for pragmatism was clearly not a forceful enough weapon against such world views; its empiricism, Beard said, burdened pragmatism with "the conservative and deadening influences of empirical servitude to habits, customs, and things experienced." As an alternative, Beard advanced what he called "the idea of civilization," which rested on "indefeasible" truths.[4]

There is also in Beard's thought a corresponding shift away from historical relativism. In 1935 Beard had declared that objective or value-free history was a "noble dream," and his own earlier work had been implicitly relativistic because of its pragmatic overtones. For example, his *Economic Interpretation of the Constitution* (1913) had suggested that although the Constitution may have been adapted to the realities of the Founding Fathers' economic interests in 1787 and was, therefore, "true" for them, it ought to be changed to meet the realities of the twentieth century, as it in fact had been by the Sixteenth, Seventeenth, and Nineteenth Amendments. In 1943, however, Beard described with approval an unchanging Constitution as a source of national unity and a safeguard against totalitarianism; he did not deny the economic motives of the Fathers but conceded that their work had been a "case of men's building better than they knew."[5]

Totalitarianism had a similar impact on Becker, as shown in his changing evaluation of the Declaration of Independence. Becker had argued in 1922 that the natural rights philosophy upon which the Declaration rested was "true" for its author Jefferson and his revolutionary colleagues only in the sense that it provided them with a rationale for independence;[6] the implication was that the document had no claim to lasting truth. In 1943, however, Becker declared that "in essentials the political philosophy of Jefferson is our political philosophy; in essentials democracy means for us what it meant for him." Clearly, Becker had reassessed the Declaration, as Beard had the Constitution, "in the light, not of the democratic ideal, but of the practical alternative exhibited for our admiration in Germany and elsewhere."[7]

The Depression at home also necessitated a rethinking of earlier Progressive assumptions about reform through pragmatic experimentation. Beard had become an advocate of a planned economy and national collectivism,[8] a course upon which Roosevelt had presumably embarked with the National Industrial Recovery Act and the Agricultural Adjustment Act in 1933. Roosevelt's reversion to the trust-busting approach to economic recovery in 1935, however, dismayed Beard.[9] Becker too was critical of New Deal economic policies, suggesting a "virtual, if not formal socialization of certain basic industries,"[10] rather than the mild regulations imposed on business by Roosevelt. Roosevelt's tendency to improvise with the economy, as in the move from the New Nationalist emphasis on planning to the New Freedom's emphasis on breaking up, rather than controlling, large economic units, indicated to these Progressives that their former belief that economic reform should adapt its methods to changing necessities was inadequate. Nevertheless, Progressives tended to see the New Deal as a continuation of their own fight for political democracy and economic equality. Roosevelt, Beard thought, combined "in his thinking the severe economic analysis of the Hamilton-Webster tradition with . . . humanistic democracy"; his major measures "looked in the direction of strengthening the economic foundations of democracy."[11]

These shifts in attitudes indicated an attempt by the Progressives to find some stable, unchanging value system in defense of democracy against totalitarianism and economic disaster.[12] However, the younger liberals accurately interpreted the move away from economic realism, from pragmatism and from historical relativism, all so intimately connected with reformist history, as the intellectual counterpart of the increasingly conservative tenor of domestic politics in the early war years. The Progressive solutions to the Depression had not worked, and the returns of the 1942 elections, defeating many New Deal legislators, indicated the country's loss of interest in substantial economic change.

Even worse, the Progressives had not relinquished their perfectionist faith in man's rational and ethical capabilities. Beard still had hopes for man's "creative intelligence" and still saw history as a "struggle of human beings in the world for individual and social perfection."[13] Becker conceded that the "liberal-democratic revolution" had not yet been accomplished, for man had not used his reason for the "humane and rational ends" that Becker desired.[14] Nevertheless, Becker's evaluation of the function of a political democracy revealed that it was, for him, still inseparably linked with man's ability to reason: "More obvious now even than in the seventeenth century is the truth of Pascal's famous dictum: 'Thought makes the whole dignity of man; therefore, endeavor to think well, that is the only morality.' The chief virtue of democracy," Becker concluded, "and in the long run the sole reason for cherishing it, is that with all its defects, it still provides the most favorable conditions for the maintenance of that dignity and the practice of that morality."[15]

Schlesinger inherited the Progressive goal of equal political participation resting upon economic equality and the Progressive method of achieving this goal through government regulation; hence his stress on the need for economic realism and on the conflict between a business class that resists government regulation and the general welfare that requires it. But he felt that the Progressives, particularly as their thought changed, were not realistic enough about the methods of achieving reform or about human nature. For Schlesinger, therefore, the more significant conflict took place within the liberal psyche itself, as this quotation from George Bancroft which appears in the preface to *The Age of Jackson* indicates:

> The feud between the capitalist and the laborer, the house of Have and the house of Want, is as old as social union, and can never be entirely quieted; but he who will act with moderation, prefer fact to theory, and remember that everything in this world is relative and not absolute, will see that the violence of the contest may be stilled.

Schlesinger's attempt to resolve the conflict between fact and theory, between relativism and absolutism, between realism and idealism, places him within the liberal camp. The "vital center" is intended to establish an inner consensus which will quell the ideological conflict without.

It is Schlesinger's reliance upon Reinhold Niebuhr's analysis of the nature of man which most sharply distinguishes Schlesinger from the Progressives. Niebuhr, Schlesinger has said, accomplished "in a single generation a revolution in the bases of American political thought. A culture which had staked too much on illusions of optimism found itself baffled and stricken in an age dominated by total government and total war."[16]

Niebuhr, himself a disillusioned former Marxist, both corrected these illusions and explained totalitarianism with his concept of original sin. Man sins, according to Niebuhr, because he realizes his finiteness in contrast with the infiniteness of God and because he has the freedom to sin. Thus, man suffers from the "anxiety [which] is the inevitable concomitant of the paradox of freedom and finiteness in which man is involved." Because he is anxious, man seeks "to over-come his insecurity by a will-to-power which over-reaches the limits of human creatureliness. Man is ignorant and involved in the limitations of a finite mind; but he pretends that he is not limited. He assumes that he can gradually transcend finite limitations until his mind becomes identical with the universal mind."[17] Man is therefore drawn to political creeds which share his illusions about his goodness and perfectibility.

Niebuhr did not refer to these philosophies as "ideologies" but as "utopias," and he labeled both Communism and liberalism as utopian.[18] Utopian philosophies, Niebuhr said, are characterized by "idealism . . . loyalty to moral norms and ideals rather than to self-interest."[19] The introduction of moral norms or absolutes into politics, he explained, arouses hopes which cannot be fulfilled; the resulting frustrations create social and political disorders such as McCarthyism.[20] The proper concern of politics is "relative peace and relative justice," for "absolutist scruples tend to increase the anarchy they abhor. That is, unfortunately, the unvarying consequence of moral absolutism in politics."[21]

In contrast, a realistic political philosophy must be based on the recognition of man's sinful nature; it must "take all factors in a social and political situation which offer resistance to established norms into account, particularly the factors of self interest and power."[22] And since man's reason is impaired, such a philosophy must be based on empiricism or experience, which is man's only reliable source of knowledge: "the problem is always to be sufficiently empirical to acknowledge the obvious facts as we experience them, even though the acknowledgement threatens the rational system by which we try to establish the coherence of things."[23] Niebuhr realized that the realistic political philosophy he described might slip into relativism. He warned, therefore, that "the recognition of historical limits must not . . . lead to a betrayal of cherished values. . . . Historical pragmatism exists on the edge of opportunism, but cannot afford to fall into the abyss."[24]

Realism and idealism were personified by Niebuhr's "children of darkness," those "moral cynics who know no law beyond their own will and interest," and the "children of light," "those who believe that self-interest should be brought under the discipline of a higher law."[25] Niebuhr's man contains within himself both light and darkness and is continually torn between their conflicting counsels. He is both victim and beneficiary of that freedom and anxiety which thrust him upward toward God and downward into sin, a "heaven-storming creature whose highest ideals are curiously compounded with his immediate and mundane interests."[26]

Niebuhr's view of the tensions between the children of darkness and the children of light provided the basis for Schlesinger's own search for the vital center. He has stressed that the liberal must be empirical and realistic, that he must not cherish illusions about himself and his fellowman lest he fall victim to ideological or utopian politics. Yet Schlesinger has also realized the need for idealism and, like Niebuhr, has sought an equilibrium between idealism and realism. Ultimately, however, Schlesinger has lost faith in both.

Schlesinger's first book, *Orestes Brownson* (1939), indicates that he then shared the Progressive belief in a political democracy based on economic equality. Brownson, the Jacksonian liberal, was a model for Schlesinger's realistic reformer: a "hard-headed [investigator] of American history in terms of economic interests," who knew that political equality depended upon economic equality. In his youth, Brownson also realized in pragmatic fashion that "logic was an incomplete guide to life" and that knowledge was to be gained from participation in practical and sometimes sordid

party politics.[27] Schlesinger contrasted Brownson's realism
with the utopianism of the Transcendentalists, who, like the
Progressives, took the "moralistic attitude toward social reform" and who "knew no sin."[28] With Brownson's conversion
to Catholicism, however, his political analysis lost its relevance and realism, for Brownson, again like the Progressives,
succumbed to the belief that "he could unravel the universe
with . . . the imperfect logic of man." Schlesinger, viewing
the failure of New Deal attempts at social planning, warned
that "logic goes by extremes, but life by compromises."[29]

Brownson was intended as an object lesson to overideal-
istic reformers, but Schlesinger solved the "problem of Richard Hildreth" in a happier way. "Hildreth . . . represented a
genuine empirical tendency of thought" and had the fore-
sight to anticipate Beard's economic interpretation of the
Constitution.[30] Hildreth was able to support Hamiltonian
fiscal policies at the same time that he held Jeffersonian democratic principles. Unlike Brownson, who veered from one ex-
treme to the other, Hildreth was a balance of realism and
idealism.

The liberalism described in *The Age of Jackson* (1945) likewise had both its realists and its idealists. Jackson himself
was a realist with a "deepening belief that the economic
problems, the balance of class power, overshadowed all other
questions of the day." His followers were equally realistic;
"the pervading insight of the Jacksonians into the relation of
democracy and a wide distribution of property kept them
from tumbling into excessive optimism over minor reforms."[31]
Again, Schlesinger pointed out the contrast, this time with
the "Utopians," who dreamed of a "golden day when all
change would come by spontaneous agreement and all men
would be brothers." In the long run, "the emotions of Utopia" were of less importance than the "tainted, corrupt, un-
satisfactory work performed by the Locofoco politicians."

And yet, Schlesinger reminded his readers, "let no one forget the generous and humane aspirations which animated the Utopian faith. Some people must dream broadly and guilelessly, if only to balance those who never dream at all."[32]

In a broader context, *The Age of Jackson* dealt with the political issues of the New Deal: the shortsightedness of the business class and the makeup of the liberal coalition of urban workers, Southern agrarians, and intellectuals. More important, it was intended to combat the ideology of laissez-faire implicit in Jeffersonian thought and to effect a reconciliation between the dreams of Jefferson, with their antistatist implications, and the realities of New Deal federal regulation. The Jeffersonians, Schlesinger said, "were operating in terms of a great common vision, strong, simple, and satisfying. . . . Yet change brought a growing divergence between the myth and the actuality," and a "century of bitter experience in the democratic fight finally led liberalism to uncover what the Jeffersonians had buried: the need for a strong government."[33] Contemporary liberalism had therefore closed the gap between myth and actuality, and Schlesinger drew the moral:

> In an age dominated by the compulsive race for easy solutions, it is well to remember that, if social catastrophe is to be avoided, it can only be by an earnest, tough-minded pragmatic attempt to wrestle with new problems as they come, without being enslaved by a theory of the past, or by a theory of the future.[34]

And so the conflict was stilled and the social catastrophe avoided, but at the price of the "great common vision" and in the name of pragmatic reality.

By 1948, however, Schlesinger felt the need for a common vision for liberalism and partially eschewed his earlier pragmatic position. He had become discouraged by Truman's inability to carry on with the economic reforms of the New Deal and by the defection of some liberals to Henry Wallace's Progressive party. "President Truman appears to have little instinct for liberalism," Schlesinger complained; "he knows the words rather than the tune." Even worse, "the sentimentalists and the utopians [in the liberal community] have turned to their wailing wall, where they innocently provide a cover for Communism."[35] Liberalism clearly needed an injection of Jeffersonian idealism to meet the ideological challenges from both the right and the left. In an attack on the "revisionist" historians who had argued that the Civil War was unnecessarily caused by the abolitionists' insistence that slavery was a moral evil, Schlesinger equated the fight against slavery with the contemporary struggle against fascism and Communism; both involved the defense of unchanging moral values on behalf of a free society. He also chided the revisionists for their optimistic or "sentimental" view of man as a rational being who could solve moral problems without the force which the United States had been compelled to use in World War II.[36] For Schlesinger, then, the current battle against the evil of Communism called for a renewed insistence upon moral values and, simultaneously, a reconsideration of man's irrational nature.

Nor could liberalism survive without theory in the "ideological conflict [which] has now detonated the power conflict."[37] Beard and Becker had earlier reached the same conclusion, but Schlesinger's answer to the problem was very different from theirs. *The Vital Center* (1949) was intended as a reexamination of the theoretical principles of a postwar liberalism which could oppose both business reaction and Communism. Schlesinger set forth here a democratic theory for a civilization in which industrialization had shattered the traditional ties of men to one another, leaving them anxious and susceptible to totalitarianism. He called for a return to the "historic philosophy of liberalism. . . . Man in its estimate is precious but not perfect. He is intoxicated by power and hence most humane in a society which distributes power widely; he is intimidated by industrialism and thus most secure in a society which will protect him from want and starvation."[38] This was hardly the "historic liberalism" of the Progressives, but one that was adapted to what Schlesinger saw as contemporary economic and psychological realities. It represented that balance which would resist ideological politics. And, Schlesinger warned, "[The] center is vital; the center must hold."[39]

The center, however, was exposed to new dangers by the ideological politics of the early fifties. Schlesinger responded by dissociating liberalism from political philosophy and moral values, which he had earlier called for, and by rejecting the Progressive goal of political democracy and economic equality which he had himself shared. First, Schlesinger was forced to defend the New Deal against McCarthy's charges that it harbored Communists who were responsible for its domestic and foreign policy.[40] In the process, however, he increasingly blurred the political distinctions between the left and the right until he was led to state that the real conservatives, the real aristocrats in the American political tradition, had been Democrats.[41] With this fusion or confusion of the philosophical identities of liberalism and conservatism, he repudiated his earlier contention that liberalism needed a firm philosophical base of its own.

Second, Schlesinger was forced to rethink his Cold War stance of the late forties, for McCarthy's attacks on containment were reinforced by the "modern ideological crusade" of General Douglas MacArthur, whose intolerance of Communism had led to his suggestion that "maximum counterforce," or atomic weaponry, be used against the Chinese Communists in Korea.[42] This crusade too closely resembled

Schlesinger's own suggestion in 1948 that moral absolutes were at stake in an all-out battle between democracy and totalitarianism. Schlesinger, therefore, now pointed out the dangers of this kind of conflict: "Relativism, it is said, inevitably leads to totalitarianism. . . . But it can be argued . . . that only those who believe in absolute values can achieve the conviction of infallibility which permits tyranny and murder. . . . Our world is more threatened by . . . absolutism than by . . . pragmatism."[43]

Third, Schlesinger redefined the problem of liberalism in the fifties as the "challenge of abundance"; the economic program of the New Deal had been all too successful, for its economic leveling had led to an anxiety-ridden mass society.[44] McCarthyism had been the result. The goal of liberalism, therefore, was not the attainment of equal political participation and equal distribution of material resources but the fostering of "individual spontaneity," or the reassertion of individuality as an antidote to a mass democracy.[45]

Schlesinger's renewed emphasis on idealism in the late fifties and early sixties reveals not only his habitual distaste for business-oriented conservatism, as illustrated by the Eisenhower era, but his loss of interest in economic reform. "Materialism—the belief that the needs of life can be fulfilled by material opulence—is not enough. It will not truly achieve for our own citizens . . . the promise of American life, for that is a moral and spiritual promise. And," he added, "it will not offer an effective counterfaith—or even an effective counterbalance—against communism."[46] The revived interest in idealism is apparent when his *Age of Roosevelt* (1957, 1959, 1960) is compared with *The Age of Jackson*. The two works have many similarities in content as well as structure,[47] for both deal with the same substantive political issues and with the intellectual climate which produced the liberal concept of the welfare state. The New Deal itself is described in the later volumes as the desired equilibrium between idealism and realism. The tensions between the first New Deal, created by "the children of light," and the second New Deal, the product of the "children of darkness," were resolved by the New Deal's occupation of the "middle ground" represented by the "Keynesian spenders." The result was a happy balance between capitalism and socialism, "which took elements from each and rendered both obsolete."[48]

But although Schlesinger had described Jackson as a realist, he saw Roosevelt as a "mixture of idealism and realism,"[49] whose "greatest resource . . . lay in his ability to stir idealism in people's souls."[50]

Philosophy also assumed a renewed importance in Schlesinger's thinking during the early sixties. In his succinct analysis of the presidential candidates of 1960, Schlesinger argued that the difference between Kennedy and Nixon was that Nixon was not identified with any political philosophy. "His appeal seems almost to reside in this very capacity for eager, unlimited flexibility," Schlesinger found. Therefore, "one may well ask: what happens to such a man in the moment of stark crisis when public issues become irreducible and nothing can meet them except a rock-bottom philosophy of politics and life?" Kennedy, on the other hand, presumably had such a philosophy. He was "an exceptionally cerebral figure. By this I mean that his attitudes proceed to an unusual degree from dispassionate rational analysis."[51]

Yet Schlesinger cautioned that the philosophy of the sixties must not be allowed to slip into ideology as had the social criticism of the Progressives, John Dewey, Beard, and Vernon Parrington; nor must idealism lapse into their brand of utopianism.[52] Therefore he carefully distinguished between idealism and ideology:

> Ideals refer to the long-run goals of a nation and the spirit in which they are pursued. Ideology is more system-

atic, more detailed, more comprehensive, more dogmat-
ic. . . . Jefferson was an expounder both of ideals and of
ideology. As an expounder of ideals, he remains a vivid
and fertile figure. . . . As an ideologist, however, Jefferson is today remote. . . . [He] believed, for example,
that agriculture was the only basis of a good society;
that the small freehold system was the only foundation
for freedom.[53]

Schlesinger went on to object to ideology because it implied
determinism, but the example of Jefferson is crucial. Jefferson represented not only laissez-faire government, or the
ideology of capitalism, but also that unrealistic faith in a participatory democracy now associated with European totalitarianism. Because these ideals were no longer congruent
with reality, Schlesinger classified them as ideological. An
ideology, then, was an obsolete ideal; conversely, an ideal
was something which, like the pragmatic concept of truth,
had no permanence and was always in flux.

The fate of the desired balance between this kind of idealism and historical reality was symbolized by Schlesinger's
concluding evaluation of Kennedy. Kennedy had represented the perfect equilibrium between fact and theory, realism and idealism; "he was a man of action who could pass
easily over to the realm of ideas and confront intellectuals
with perfect confidence in his capacity to hold his own."
Since he was neither "utopian" nor "ideological," Kennedy
was both a "conservative" and a "progressive."[54] (Schlesinger referred to himself in this book as both a "liberal idealist" and "an historian and therefore a conservative."[55]) The
balance was destroyed by Lee Harvey Oswald on November 22, 1963, and, writing after Kennedy's assassination,
Schlesinger was forced to reevaluate the possibilities of the
vital center or the tenuous consensus he had sought in contemporary America. What he saw now was the "fragility of
the membranes of a civilization stretched so thin over a na-

tion so disparate in its composition, so tense in its interior relationships, so cunningly enmeshed in underground fears and antagonisms, so entrapped in the ethos of violence"[56] that the balance would inevitably be destroyed, and the conflict, temporarily smothered, would not be stilled.

Given Schlesinger's assumptions, however, the balance or the inner consensus between realism and Schlesinger's idealism was impossible of fulfillment. In his attempt to divorce idealism from the ideology associated with Progressive perfectionism or utopianism, Schlesinger made idealism synonymous with reality; both were ever-changing and ever-dependent upon historical circumstances. This led to the very ideology he wished to avoid. For thirty years, Schlesinger has told liberals to confront reality. However, during this period, the reality has changed from economic deprivation to mass society and finally to violence. Indeed, he has emphasized that the "one constant in history is change,"[57] as is illustrated by his own constantly changing definition of liberalism. But how is the liberal to be "realistic" in this situation? Just as Niebuhr argued that irrational man will cling to absolutes in the face of change because absolutes provide him with the certainty he craves, so Schlesinger feared in *The Vital Center* that modern industrialism had created conditions of social instability and disequilibrium which would drive man to seek security in totalitarian ideology.[58] Therefore, given a theory of history whose chief characteristics are flux and change, Schlesinger's liberal must necessarily succumb to ideology, and his plea for "realism" is hardly realistic.

On the other hand, it is equally difficult, under these same conditions, for the liberal to be an idealist. Since idealism has no lasting hold on truth, yesterday's ideals are today's ideologies, as he has shown us in the case of Jefferson. With reality ever-changing, then, idealism will inevitably degenerate into ideology, and the idealist, like Jefferson, will become the ideologist. Schlesinger himself falls into this trap of ethical relativism, for although the Kennedy administration is described as nonideological, it is not interested in any of the issues which Schlesinger himself had earlier identified with idealism: the struggle against capitalism and against Communism.[59] Schlesinger, therefore, finds himself in the same camp as Jefferson.

Supposing, however, for the sake of the argument, that a realistic empiricist could survive in this chaotic universe, how would he react to this constant change? Schlesinger has given us two examples. The first is Orestes Brownson, who "possessed a rare sensitivity to the hard and obstinate facts which lie in wait for theory." Consequently, "one event after another left its imprint on his thought."[60] The second is the pragmatic Franklin Roosevelt, who, in the period between the first and second New Deals, "as usual . . . avoided ideological commitment. As usual, he even avoided intellectual clarity." The result, Schlesinger concluded, was that "events . . . impose[d] policy on him."[61] One might ask then of the realistic liberal, as Schlesinger did of the ever-wavering Nixon in 1960, "what happens to such a man in the moment of stark crisis?"[62] This kind of liberal appears to be not so much attuned to facts as at their mercy.

The fate of the hypothetical idealist is slightly different, though hardly more cheerful. Like Niebuhr, Schlesinger believes that knowledge is gained through experience and particularly through political power. However, again like Niebuhr, Schlesinger believes that power inevitably corrupts. In his description of the two strains of American reform, for example, he posed the alternatives: the pragmatist accepts power and is corrupted; the utopian rejects it and is irrelevant.[63] The idealistic liberal must then choose between the evils of guilt and futility.

Schlesinger ultimately has no solution to the problem of the liberal. In his advocacy of the "middle way" out of the Vietnam War, he relinquished the one realm, foreign policy, in which he had consistently argued that morality was important.[64] When Schlesinger admitted that the actual determines the ideal, morality became defined in terms of the possible:[65] there could be no more causes worth fighting for, no more just wars like the Civil War. On the other hand, his belief that attention to the realities of American life would yield answers was first shaken by John Kennedy's assassination, then shattered by the murders of Robert Kennedy and Martin Luther King. Schlesinger could only conclude,

> Our commitment to morality, our faith in experiment: these have been the sources of America's greatness, but they have also led Americans into . . . error. For our moralists have sometimes condoned murder if the cause is deemed good. . . . And our pragmatists have sometimes ignored the means if the result is what they want. Moralism and pragmatism have not provided infallible restraints on the destructive instinct.[66]

But what other options has he ever given the liberal?

When the violence and conflict of ideological politics which have always lurked below the surface of Schlesinger's thought become the reality, the precarious balance and consensus which he sought for the liberal is destroyed. Schlesinger, like Yeats, must face the reality that when an irrational man faces an irrational universe, "Things fall apart; the center cannot hold; / Mere anarchy is loosed upon the world."

## NOTES

1. Richard Hofstadter, *The Progressive Historians: Turner, Beard, and Parrington* (New York: Alfred A. Knopf, 1968), p. 438; John Higham et al., *History* (Englewood Cliffs, N.J.: Prentice-Hall, 1965), p. 212; J. Rogers Hollingsworth, "Consensus and Continuity in Recent American Historical Writing," *South Atlantic Quarterly* 61 (Winter, 1962): 49. On Schlesinger as a conservative, see Kenneth McNaught, "American Progressives and the Great Society," *Journal of American History* 53 (December, 1966): 504–20.
2. Carl L. Becker, *Everyman His Own Historian: Essays on History and Politics* (Chicago: Quadrangle Books, 1966), pp. 114–31.
3. Charles A. Beard, *The American Spirit: A Study of the Idea of Civilization in the United States* (New York: Macmillan Co., 1942), p. 4.
4. Ibid., pp. 671–72.
5. *The Republic: Conversations on Fundamentals* (New York: Viking Press, 1943), p. 3.
6. *The Declaration of Independence: A Study in the History of Political Ideas* (New York: Vintage Books, 1960), p. 277.
7. "What Is Still Living in the Political Philosophy of Thomas Jefferson," in *Detachment and the Writing of History: Essays and Letters of Carl L. Becker*, ed. Phil L. Snyder (Ithaca: Cornell University Press, 1958), p. 239.
8. Arthur A. Ekirch, Jr., *Ideologies and Utopias: The Impact of the New Deal on American Thought* (Chicago: Quadrangle Books, 1969), p. 130.
9. Arthur M. Schlesinger, Jr., *The Age of Roosevelt*, vol. 3, *The Politics of Upheaval* (Boston: Houghton Mifflin Co., 1960), pp. 151–54, 390.
10. *Modern Democracy* (New Haven: Yale University Press, 1941), p. 91.
11. Charles A. Beard and Mary R. Beard, *America in Mid-Passage* (New York: Macmillan Co., 1939), p. 947.

12. Cushing Strout, *The Pragmatic Revolt in American History: Carl Becker and Charles Beard* (New Haven: Yale University Press, 1958), pp. 41, 116, and passim; Higham, *History*, pp. 206–7.

13. *The American Spirit*, pp. 671, 672.

14. *Modern Democracy*, pp. 33, 98.

15. Ibid., p. 100.

16. "Theology and Politics from the Social Gospel to the Cold War: The Impact of Reinhold Niebuhr," in *Intellectual History in America: From Darwin to Niebuhr*, ed. Cushing Strout (New York: Harper and Row, 1968), vol. 2, p. 180.

17. Harry R. Davis and Robert C. Good, eds., *Reinhold Niebuhr on Politics: His Political Philosophy and Its Application to Our Age as Expressed in His Writings* (New York: Charles Scribner's Sons, 1960), p. 77.

18. Ibid., pp. 13–40.

19. Reinhold Niebuhr, *Christian Realism and Political Problems* (New York: Charles Scribner's Sons, 1953), p. 120.

20. "The Cause and Cure of American Psychosis," *American Scholar* 25 (Winter, 1955–56): 11–20.

21. "Pacifism Against the Wall," *American Scholar* 2 (Spring, 1936): 141.

22. *Christian Realism*, pp. 119–20.

23. *Pious and Secular America* (New York: Charles Scribner's Sons, 1958), p. 127.

24. *The Irony of American History* (New York: Charles Scribner's Sons, 1952), p. 143.

25. *The Children of Light and the Children of Darkness: A Vindication of Democracy and a Critique of Its Traditional Defense* (New York: Charles Scribner's Sons, 1944), p. 9.

26. Davis and Good, *Reinhold Niebuhr on Politics*, p. 62.

27. *Orestes Brownson: A Pilgrim's Progress* (Boston: Little, Brown and Co., 1939), pp. 116, 26.

28. Ibid., pp. 38, 150.

29. Ibid., p. 291.
30. "The Problem of Richard Hildreth," *New England Quarterly* 13 (June, 1940): 234.
31. *The Age of Jackson* (Boston: Little, Brown and Co., 1950), pp. 59, 344.
32. Ibid., pp. 362–66, 368.
33. Ibid., pp. 512, 519.
34. Ibid., p. 522.
35. "Political Culture in the United States," *The Nation* 166 (March 13, 1948): 308.
36. "The Causes of the Civil War: A Note on Historical Sentimentalism," *Partisan Review* 16 (1949): 969–81.
37. *The Vital Center: The Politics of Freedom* (Boston: Houghton Mifflin Co., 1949), p. 9.
38. Ibid., p. 156.
39. Ibid., p. 255.
40. For example, "Whittaker Chambers and His 'Witness,'" *Saturday Review* 35 (May 24, 1952): 8–10, 39–41.
41. "The New Conservatism: The Politics of Conservatism," *Reporter* 12 (June 16, 1955): 11; "The New Conservatism in America: A Liberal Comment," *Confluence* 2 (December, 1953): 68.
42. Richard H. Rovere and Arthur M. Schlesinger, Jr., *The General and the President and the Future of American Foreign Policy* (New York: Farrar, Straus, and Young, 1951), p. 225.
43. "Whittaker Chambers," p. 41.
44. "Death Wish of the Democrats," *New Republic* 139 (September 15, 1958): 9; "The Future of Liberalism: The Challenge of Abundance," *Reporter* 14 (May 3, 1956): 8–9.
45. *The Politics of Hope* (Boston: Houghton Mifflin Co., 1963), p. 244.
46. Ibid., p. 83.
47. Marcus Cunliffe, "Arthur M. Schlesinger, Jr.," in *Pastmasters: Some Essays on American Historians*, ed. Marcus

Cunliffe and Robin W. Winks (New York: Harper and Row, 1969), pp. 354, 364.

48. *The Politics of Upheaval*, pp. 398, 401, 651.

49. *The Age of Roosevelt*, vol. 1, *The Crisis of the Old Order*, p. 331.

50. *The Age of Roosevelt*, vol. 2, *The Coming of the New Deal*, p. 557.

51. *Kennedy or Nixon: Does It Make Any Difference?* (New York: Macmillan Co., 1960), pp. 3–4, 18, 23–24.

52. "Sources of the New Deal," in *Paths of American Thought*, ed. Arthur M. Schlesinger, Jr., and Morton White (Boston: Houghton Mifflin Co., 1963), pp. 376–77, 381.

53. "The One Against the Many," ibid., pp. 533–34. This appeared originally in *Saturday Review*, July 14, 1962; copyright 1962 by Saturday Review, Inc.

54. *A Thousand Days: John F. Kennedy in the White House* (Boston: Houghton Mifflin Co., 1965), pp. 104, 112.

55. Ibid., pp. 129, 135.

56. Ibid., pp. 724–25.

57. "The Right Man for the Big Job," *New York Times Magazine*, April 3, 1960, p. 120.

58. *The Vital Center*, pp. 243–44.

59. *A Thousand Days*, pp. 298–99, 609–10.

60. *Orestes Brownson*, p. 281.

61. *The Politics of Upheaval*, pp. 263–64.

62. *Kennedy or Nixon*, p. 18.

63. "The Administration and the Left," *New Statesman* 65 (February 8, 1963): 185.

64. "A Middle Way Out of Vietnam," *New York Times Magazine*, September 18, 1966, pp. 47–48, 111–20; "The Causes of the Civil War: A Note on Historical Sentimentalism," *Partisan Review* 16 (1949): 969–81; "Adding Guns to E.C.A. Butter," *New Republic* 119 (November 22, 1948): 19–21; "Roosevelt and His Detractors," *Harper's* 200 (June, 1950): 62–68.

65. Arthur M. Schlesinger, Jr., Lewis A. Coser, Oscar Gass,

and Hans Morgenthau, "America and the World Revolution," *Commentary* 36 (October, 1963): 293.

66.  "The Dark Heart of American History," *Saturday Review* 51 (October 19, 1968): 21.

# CHAPTER 3

# *LOUIS HARTZ AND THE SEARCH FOR IDENTITY*

Louis Hartz has provided a forceful analysis of the uniqueness of American political thought and is probably the most quoted source on the liberal consensus. Until recently, his contention that Locke was the one significant source of American political theory was generally accepted, and Hartz' argument that there has been overwhelming agreement on Lockean values has stimulated much empirical work.[1] His concept of the liberal consensus, however, has retained much of its academic vitality because it is ambiguous. The thesis that we are all liberals has been cited as the basis of the "new conservatism" of the 1950's and simultaneously as proof that the quest for a new conservatism is futile; it has also been used to deflate the radicalism of reformers by describing them as unconscious Lockean conservatives and to establish the legitimacy of reform radicalism within the Lockean framework.[2] This confusion stems not only from what appears to be the studied obscurity of Hartz' prose, but also from the fact that he has been engaged in a persistent and evolving pursuit of an identity for the liberal which would, ultimately, shield him from the ideological politics of Europe.

Hartz is best known for his criticism in *The Liberal Tradition in America* (1955) of the wedding of that tradition to the obsolete values of private property and laissez-faire capitalism, the ideology attacked by the Progressives. Like Schle-

51

singer's *Vital Center*, however, Hartz' book was also a criticism of pragmatism and the lack of a rational and realistic liberal theory. Following Roosevelt's death in 1945, pragmatism came under fire because its hostility toward formalized systems of thought had apparently contributed to the collapse of liberal reform. Roosevelt's improvisations with the economy now seemed to have left his successor Truman with no clear-cut direction or goal, as he scrapped price controls in 1946 and threatened to draft railroad workers striking against the resulting inflation. The Taft-Hartley Bill indicated a new hostility to the organized labor movement stimulated by New Deal measures, just as the Republican leadership of Robert Taft revealed the desire of the American public, exhausted by New Deal reformism and wartime hardships, to return to normalcy. Liberals conjectured that had Roosevelt relied less on pragmatic trial and error and more on intellectually consistent premises based on defined liberal values, a cohesive liberal reform force might have retained wartime controls on the economy, curbing free enterprise and moving the country in the direction of a more thoroughgoing overhaul of the economic status quo. The splintering of the Democratic coalition in 1948 reinforced this feeling. Truman could not hold together the strange bedfellows of the New Deal alliance; Strom Thurmond and the Dixiecrats were offended by Truman's liberalism, and Henry Wallace and the Progressives, by his conservatism. No effective challenge to capitalism could be mounted by a liberalism so disunited.

The lack of a liberal philosophy also made liberalism seem vulnerable to the ideology of perfectionism both abroad and at home. Liberal pragmatism had allowed the United States to join forces with the Soviet Union, which had now turned upon its deliverer as Stalin broke the promises made at Yalta and rejected the Baruch plan for international control of atomic weaponry. The Truman Doctrine, although intended to meet the new Soviet menace, in effect aided reactionary regimes abroad, as in Greece, simply because they were anti-Communist. Moreover, United States aid to these governments was primarily economic and military and did not provide the forces of democracy with the moral or intellectual dynamism needed in the Cold War battle for men's minds.

Nor could liberalism successfully combat the ideology of perfectionism at home, as indicated by liberal support of Wallace's Communist-backed Progressive party. A prominent New Dealer for fourteen years and Vice-President during Roosevelt's third term, Wallace ran on a platform representing liberal desires of the early 1940's: a measure of national collectivism and an internationalism which rested on renewed rapport with the Soviet Union. Truman had fired Wallace in 1946 from his Cabinet post after Wallace had attacked the belligerence of Truman's policy toward the Soviet Union, but this stance made him attractive to Communists and to those liberals who were still fellow-traveling. Wallace was by no means the political threat he appeared to be, as the 1948 election returns showed, but the efforts of the Americans for Democratic Action to persuade the conservative Eisenhower to run as the Democratic candidate revealed their fears that Wallace's leftism still exercised great appeal to the liberal community.

Clearly, the pragmatism of the early 1940's, inherited from but already disavowed by the Progressives, had failed. Liberalism had placed too much faith in man's reason; a philosophy was necessary to remind liberals of man's fallibility and to prevent their capitulation to the ideologies of capitalism and perfectionism.

This disillusion with liberalism's earlier pragmatism was reflected in much of the liberal literature of the late forties and early fifties. Political scientists like James McGregor

Burns, critical of pragmatism in political practice, urged the use of party discipline to enforce definitive party policies; this would correct the existing loosely knit national parties and prevent party schisms like that of 1948. The same case for party government was made by the Committee on Political Parties of the American Political Science Association in 1950.[3]

Morton White's *Social Thought in America* (1949) directly attributed to pragmatism the collapse of postwar liberalism. Although sympathetic to the humanitarianism of John Dewey, James Harvey Robinson, and Charles Beard, White found that their "revolt against formalism" had resulted in "liberalism's anxiety about having principles turn into dogma." "Today," he mourned, "we have little to choose from except the despair of those who are no longer interested, the cynicism of others who continue to call themselves liberals but who have surrendered their consciences, the nonsense of shameless defenders of reaction in the name of revolution."[4] Eric Goldman voiced the same concern in his *Rendezvous with Destiny* (1952). Goldman acknowledged his own personal debt to Beard and admitted that the belief that "all ideas must be submitted to the pragmatic test" had been a useful weapon against conservatism. But, he implied, the lack of absolute standards and of intellectual clarity inherent in the pragmatic position had permitted liberals to become Communists or Popular Fronters during the 1930's,[5] a reference to those naïvely optimistic liberals who supported Wallace.

These doubts about an overoptimistic and intellectually flabby liberalism were echoed by Lionel Trilling. In an early statement of the consensus position, he declared that "in the United States at this time [1949] liberalism is not only the dominant but even the sole intellectual tradition." This tradition he found intellectually bankrupt, however, lacking "the authority, the cogency, the completeness, the brilliance, the hardness of systematic thought." What was needed to shake liberalism out of its complacency, Trilling suggested, was a powerful and articulate conservative philosophy which would cause liberalism to reexamine its premises and "recall [it] to its first essential imagination of variousness and possibility, which implies the awareness of complexity and difficulty."[6]

Hartz' work must be seen as an attempt to remind liberals of the complexity and difficulty of reform. Like Schlesinger, Hartz described the liberal as a personality split between realism and idealism. Seeking both a diagnosis and a cure for this divided personality, Hartz relied upon Erich Fromm's explanation of ideological politics in totalitarian Europe. Fromm's *Escape from Freedom* (1941) was primarily an analysis of the psychosocial setting of Hitler's Germany. With the disintegration of the tightly knit medieval society and the emergence of modern individualism, Fromm said, man became at once more free and more alone. Unable to cope with this isolation, he had sought security and identity either by succumbing to a totalitarian ideology like fascism or Communism, or through "the compulsive conforming [that] is prevalent in our own democracy,"[7] which Fromm saw as a peculiarly American form of totalitarianism. Man has a basic need for identity, but capitalism, by subordinating man's individuality to material gain, makes him merely a "cog in the vast economic machine."[8] A capitalist society also fosters loss of identity by glorifying man's intellect at the expense of his emotions. Since man must have emotional outlets, Fromm said, there is in our culture "the readiness to accept any ideology and any leader if only he promises excitement and offers a political structure and symbols which allegedly give meaning and order to an individual's life. The despair of the human automaton is fertile soil for the political purposes of Fascism."[9]

Fromm offered two solutions for this loss of identity. The first was reform of the capitalist system, illustrated by the communitarian socialism he described in *The Sane Society*.[10] The second was a change in man's spiritual and philosophical orientation; every man by himself, Fromm said, should be the source of his own values, for his salvation lay in "self-love . . . the affirmation of his truly human self."[11] Fromm denied that his humanistic concept of self-love was inevitably relativistic, for he argued that through the use of reason, and specifically through psychology, man can discover certain "objective" norms to guide his behavior.[12]

For Fromm, therefore, man's reason, although imperfect, was essential to his full development. Unreasoning conformity may bring security, Fromm maintained, but "free man is by necessity insecure; thinking man by necessity uncertain."[13] Fromm's goal was the harmony between reason and emotion necessary for man to find his true identity and real freedom: "positive freedom consists in the spontaneous activity of the total, integrated personality . . . [in] the acceptance of the total person and the elimination of the split between 'reason' and 'nature.' "[14]

Hartz' quest has been for the identity of this "total, integrated personality" which would combat the liberal susceptibility to ideological politics. His first book, *Economic Policy and Democratic Thought* (1948), described the split between reason and nature which he would later attempt to heal. Like Schlesinger's *Age of Jackson*, this study of the controversy in nineteenth-century Pennsylvania over state control of private enterprise was concerned with the intellectual and historical antecedents of the most pressing issue of the

Depression period—American adherence to the ideology of laissez-faire, given new impetus by World War II.

Hartz indicated at the outset of the book his indebtedness to the Progressive goal of a participatory democracy resting on economic equality; as early as the American Revolution, he said, "economic control [of private corporations] and political democracy became sister principles of the Radical position." Of these, political democracy became the more potent force and "gave to the theory of economic policy its color and vitality."[15] Despite its power, however, political democracy did not rest upon a realistic assessment of the nature of the individual and of the community, the two main concepts upon which it was based.[16] The belief in the primacy of the individual did dictate some reforms such as debtor legislation and abolition.[17] But the reform tendencies of individualism were all too easily overridden by man's inherent selfishness and degenerated into acquisitiveness and the "glorification of property rights"[18] associated with the ideology of capitalism. Equally unrealistic was the notion of the community, which rested upon the assumption of a "unified and infallible popular will."[19] The reality, as Hartz saw it, was not unity but conflict between sectional and economic interests.

Because they were unrealistic, these two concepts of democratic theory could be seized upon by the conservative opponents of state regulation in the post-Civil War period and were used to support laissez-faire economics. Hartz' conclusions were critical of the halfway measures of New Deal liberalism, the legacy of this perversion of democratic theory:

> In this new world of doctrine . . . businessmen were heroes and politicians were villains, a balanced budget was the mark of state morality, and the menace of com-

munism was ground for constitutional argument. It was
an excellent set of symbols for the task at hand: the
substitution of the concept of negative for the concept
of positive government.[20]

Of greater importance, the "unrealism of democratic ideals"
or the "gap between myth and fact"[21] stood in the way of
genuine economic reform.

*Economic Policy and Democratic Thought* was a criticism
of the ideology of capitalism and of Progressive perfectionism. As for Schlesinger in *The Age of Jackson*, pragmatic reform for Hartz must have an economic rather than a theoretical basis.

*The Liberal Tradition* revealed a change of heart, for here
Hartz argued that liberalism was weakened by its reliance
on the pragmatic method and that an articulated philosophy
was necessary to close that gap between fact and myth he
had earlier described. The liberal was referred to as "Horatio
Alger," the "democratic capitalist," indicating again the division between democratic theory and economic reality; he was
a blend of Jefferson's faith in the people and the Whig
"capitalist dream."[22] In an obvious reference to the dissolution of the Democratic party in 1948, Hartz declared that
the liberal was "never quite sure whether he was an 'aristo-
crat,' a farmer, or an urban worker."[23] The intellectual counterpart of that political fragmentation was that "American
political thought . . . is a veritable maze of polar contradictions, winding in and out of each other hopelessly: pragmatism and absolutism, historicism and rationalism, optimism
and pessimism, materialism and idealism, individualism and
conformism."[24] He summed up these contradictions in his
term "Lockeanism," a form of intellectual shorthand referring both to John Locke's belief in popular sovereignty rest-

ing upon the right of revolution and to his theory that property ownership is the basis of society.

Lockean values were once congruent with the uniqueness of the American environment, "the distinctive element in American civilization: its social freedom, its social equality."[25] These conditions had changed, but Americans remained Lockeans; therefore, Hartz classified Lockeanism as an ideology, explaining the hold of this anachronistic seventeenth-century philosophy on the American mind in terms of Fromm's analysis of totalitarianism. The "atomistic social freedom" and isolation from Europe, exemplified by the lack of feudal traditions in this country, created this susceptibility to ideology: the "psychic heritage of a nation 'born free' is . . . a colossal liberal absolutism."[26] Just as Fromm's contemporary man, in his anguished aloneness, sought security in totalitarian creeds and conformity, Hartz' American, fleeing the burden of freedom, found refuge in the ideology of Locke and the stifling conformity Hartz called "Americanism."

The results of this unanimous endorsement of Locke were unfortunate. The emphasis on property, fostered by the material abundance of nature in the New World, thwarted any attempts to curb economic individualism. Hartz pointed out that even the Progressives and the New Dealers clung to outmoded capitalism. Locke's concept of the right of revolution, which lent support to the democratic theory of political participation, was equally ideological, for it had no basis in American reality. The American Revolution had in fact been conservative because there had been no feudal traditions to overthrow. The failure of the Progressives, therefore, lay also in their inability to see that the American liberal was not a revolutionary democrat but a conservative property

owner: Progressives saw a conflict between "conservatism" and "radicalism" that simply did not exist.[27] The
Progressive belief that the liberal could or would change his
institutions was folly, as the survival of free enterprise
proved. Further, the lack of a real revolutionary philosophy
was a handicap in the revolutionary setting of the Cold
War,[28] and the American effort to combat Communism had
simply led to the support of another variety of totalitarianism, as had the Truman Doctrine in Greece.

Like Fromm, therefore, Hartz argued that this schizo-
phrenic liberal could find his true identity by integrating nature and reason; democratic theory must correspond to the
economic and psychological realities of this century. His
hope was that contact with the world community, bringing
an end to American uniqueness and isolation, would provide
a "spark of philosophy"[29] to help the American discover his
real identity within this larger context.

Published after the McCarthy furor had begun, however,
*The Liberal Tradition* was a transitional book, foreshadow-
ing later liberal thought. For despite his plea for a new philosophy or identity, Hartz pointed out that the side of Locke
represented by the American devotion to private property
was "too real, too empirical, too historical in America to attack"; the alternative to capitalism offered by the "Southern
feudalists" was "fantasy."[30] Despite its conservatism, this
side of liberalism was rooted in the material realities of life
on this continent; the side of Horatio Alger represented by
the "man of the land, [the] small capitalist in the backwoods"
and the "independent entrepreneur" fitted the facts of the
American environment.[31] Moreover, although critical,
Hartz' contention that we are all liberals blurred the distinctions between the political left and right much as Schlesinger
had done in the early fifties. Hartz also noted that although
the New Deal had no guiding philosophy, it had worked; in

short, it was not clear whether he was lamenting or rejoicing that the "dreamers . . . in American history" have been the victims of America's "unconquerable pragmatism."[32]

Hartz' position was clarified in subsequent writings, for when McCarthy led the people in rebellion against the status quo, Hartz' belief that Horatio Alger the democrat could not overthrow his institutions appeared incorrect; the Progressives had been right about Alger's revolutionary potential. Hartz' later attempts to close the gap between democratic theory and economic reality made explicit his rejection of his own appeal for a liberal philosophy and of the Progressive ideal of a participatory democracy. In 1952 Hartz declared that politics was the "pulling and hauling of interest" or "logrolling"; for "in politics most principles break down when carried to their 'logical conclusion.' " Principles such as he and his fellow liberals had earlier advocated were not only irrelevant but a perilous guide to political behavior; "the most dangerous moment in the political life of any community [is] the moment of almost perfect rationalization of its internal conflict."[33]

In a discussion of the "image and reality" of democracy, Hartz found that the Jeffersonian image of a participatory democracy did not square with the "group coercion, crowd psychology and economic power" which had always been the real stuff of politics. He then linked democratic theory with the perfectionist ideologies of European totalitarianism: "these ideologies are utopian" and, like democratic theory, raise hopes too high and create disenchantment and disaster. We must have a more realistic notion of democracy, he said, lest it become equated with utopia.[34]

Hartz did not deny that democracy involved participation by its citizens. In fact, he found in the American a "genius for political participation,"[35] but he viewed this participation as a conditioned response to a particular stimulus, not a rational act. This stimulus was the "liberal idea," as Hartz now redefined it: at its root was "land hunger and economic ambition," with Locke as its symbol.[36] The "idea" which now motivated the liberal was in reality economic self-interest. Thus, Hartz concluded, "one may oppose [the millionaire's] dream and find it unsuitable as a way of life, but it was an inherent manifestation of the democratic idea."[37] Democracy had become the process by which self-interested man competed for economic benefits when Locke, the dual source of perfectionism and capitalism, was replaced by Locke, the source of capitalism alone.

In *The Founding of New Societies* (1964) Hartz introduced the new American liberal invulnerable to ideology. The book is a comparison of the intellectual development of five colonial or "fragment" cultures, including the American fragment, which Hartz described as "bourgeois." The key to this development was the psychological premise set forth in *The Liberal Tradition*: "Being part of a whole is psychologically tolerable, but being merely a part isolated from a whole is not. It is obvious that there is a major problem of self-definition inherent in the process of fragmentation."[38] Again, this problem of "self-definition" or identity resulted in the fragment's flight to absolutism and conformity; again, there was the distinctive lack of political philosophy.

The insular life of the fragment was doomed, however; contact with Europe and European ideologies was inevitable. Yet, "as the fragment world passes," Hartz mourned, "even a critic of its values cannot fail to have a nostalgic pang." He then discovered, however, that the American fragment was no longer internally divided, as he had described it earlier, for Andrew Jackson had been the "messenger . . . of national completeness. . . . [D]uring the Middle Period of American history . . . all Americans . . . were 'forgetting' Europe together, becoming Americans." They had, therefore, found an identity in that "peculiar American amalgam of individualist, democratic, and capitalist intensities out of which Alger emerges," "a blending of the two great traditions of the national history: Hamilton and Jefferson."[39] Wholeness, or identity, however, has been found in 1964 only after the participatory democracy of Jefferson had been transformed into the "capitalist dream."

Alger, not surprisingly, was a political conservative and something of an elitist; he was "not an alienated figure suddenly hurled to power," but a sober fellow who had "belonged before, and his exhilaration was therefore kept in bounds."[40] Life inside the fragment was secure, although this very security smothered philosophy. In fact, it was apparent that this security was made possible by the very absence of philosophy which Hartz ostensibly deplored. "The 'participative rationality' of the average voter preclude[d] . . . the theoretical rationality of the intelligentsia. . . . [T]hat participative rationality, bred of the liberal tradition, is not always the fount of critical enlightenment. But this situation is at the heart of American democratic success."[41]

Hartz had seen during the McCarthy period that his own demand for an identity or philosophy had brought "deepening insecurity and . . . fantastic anxieties."[42] Furthermore, the return of the fragment to the larger world, he now said, introduced "an element of 'freedom' into a pattern historically determined" by providing a choice of alternative ideologies which the fragment did not initially have. And "it is only when [the fragment's] containment is shattered by external experience, and objectivity begins to appear, that determinism is converted into choice. That of course is what is happening today."[43]

Yet Hartz was evidently afraid that the liberal could not survive the loss of his peculiarly American identity—perhaps because the "spark of philosophy" from the larger world might ignite the irrationality lurking beneath the placid surface of the American citizenry; perhaps because the escape from determinism which a new identity would bring would simply precipitate another and more disastrous escape from freedom. The old uniqueness, the familiar identity, was the safer bet, and the American liberal emerged triumphantly as Horatio Alger, the self-seeking capitalist.

The bases of this evaluation of American liberalism in 1964 were implicit in Hartz' first book, for there the myth of democracy and democratic theory was contrasted with the reality of economics and man's economic self-interest. However, if Hartz in 1948 lamented certain aspects of American life, he now appeared to celebrate them. He no longer maintained, as he had in *Economic Policy and Democratic Thought*, that the capitalist ethos was incompatible with democracy; to the contrary, it now appeared that the success of democracy rested upon capitalism. This position was necessitated by his fear that democratic theory had become linked with the perfectionist ideologies of Europe; American uniqueness, therefore, rested solely upon the American institution of capitalism.

Initially, the total identity of the liberal was intended to shield him from both capitalism and perfectionism. Although this identity was to be achieved through an integration of reason and nature, reason was to provide the guide to man's behavior, as it was for Fromm and as was illustrated in Hartz' plea for a liberal philosophy. Alger, though, does not represent an integration of reason, represented by democratic ideals, and nature, represented by economic reality. For just as Schlesinger achieved the balanced liberal by making idealism and realism synonymous, Alger, without the myth or vision of Jefferson's democracy, is no longer the democratic capitalist, but simply the capitalist. Hartz, in short, by eschewing the ideals of perfectionism, has capitulated to the realities of capitalism.

This liberal cannot be the reformer Hartz originally envisioned, for unlike Fromm's reasoning man, Alger cannot bring about change. Like the Lockeanism from which he springs, he is "too real, too empirical, too historical"; he is the personification of that "liberal idea" created by the "magnificent material setting of the New World."[44] Therefore, although Hartz used a comparative approach in *The Founding of New Societies* so that the American could "[master] rather than [project] the absolutism of his flight from Europe," he was simultaneously pessimistic about this possibility: "To ask that the American fragment . . . become master of its own consciousness, objective about its life and origin, is obviously to ask more than normal cultural determinism will permit."[45] Thus, Alger has gained an identity but only by escaping from freedom.

Alger, moreover, represents that side of Locke which Hartz identified not only with the natural environment but, by implication, with Locke's theory of the state of nature, in which the rule was every man for himself. Hartz himself saw in 1948 that Alger's individualism readily became transformed into the "glorification of property rights"; Alger's self-love, unlike Fromm's, is unrestrained by love of others. This self-interested liberal is unlikely to part with his property to further that economic justice necessary for political democracy.

Nor could this liberal ever have formulated the "realistic" intellectual weapons for reform that Hartz desired. The reality, for Hartz, has always been economics and man's self-aggrandizing nature; in this context, disinterested political participation is nonrational or irrational, for the political process is the method by which each man takes care of his own material welfare. For the citizens of this democracy, ideals are myths, and the millionaire's dream becomes the liberal philosophy.

## NOTES

1.  See David W. Minar, *Ideas and Politics: The American Experience* (Homewood, Ill.: Dorsey Press, 1964), esp. p. 64; or William T. Bluhm, *Theories of the Political System: Classics of Political Thought and Modern Political Analysis* (Englewood Cliffs, N.J.: Prentice-Hall, 1965), pp. 300–329, on the dominance of Locke in American political thought. For examples of attempts to validate the consensus theory with empirical data, see Herbert McCloskey, "Consensus and Ideology in American Politics," *American Political Science Review* 58 (June, 1964): 361–82; or James W. Prothro and Charles M. Grigg, "Fundamental Principles of Democracy: Bases of Agreement and Disagreement," *Journal of Politics* 22 (Spring, 1960): 276–94.

2.  William J. Newman, *The Futilitarian Society* (New York: Braziller, 1961), pp. 300–327; Bernard Crick, "The Strange Quest for an American Conservatism," *The Review of Politics* 17 (July, 1953): 359–76; Lee Benson, *The Concept of Jacksonian Democracy: New York as a Test Case* (Princeton: Princeton University Press, 1961), esp. pp. 272–77; Marvin Meyers, *The Jacksonian Persuasion: Politics and Belief* (Stanford: Stanford University Press, 1968), esp. p. 243; Michael Paul Rogin, *The Intellectuals and McCarthy: The Radical Spectre* (Cambridge, Mass., and London: M.I.T. Press, 1967), pp. 35–41.

3.  James McGregor Burns, *Congress on Trial: The Legislative Process and the Administrative State* (New York: Harper and Bros., 1949); American Political Science Association, "Towards a More Responsible Two-Party System: A Report of the Committee on Political Parties," Supplement to *American Political Science Review* 44 (September, 1950).

4.  *Social Thought in America: The Revolt Against Formalism* (New York: Viking Press, 1949), pp. 241–42.

5.  *Rendezvous with Destiny: A History of Modern American Reform* (New York: Vintage Books, 1958), pp. 154, 277.

6.  *The Liberal Imagination: Essays on Literature and Society* (Garden City, N.Y.: Doubleday and Co., 1957), pp. vii, 280, xii.
7.  *Escape from Freedom* (New York and Toronto: Rinehart and Co., 1941), p. 62.
8.  Ibid., p. 110.
9.  Ibid., p. 256.
10. *The Sane Society* (New York and Toronto: Rinehart and Co., 1955), pp. 270–352.
11. *Man for Himself: An Inquiry into the Psychology of Ethics* (Greenwich, Conn.: Fawcett Publications, 1956), p. 17.
12. Ibid., p. vii.
13. *The Sane Society*, pp. 196–97.
14. *Escape from Freedom*, pp. 258–59.
15. *Economic Policy and Democratic Thought: Pennsylvania, 1776–1860* (Cambridge: Harvard University Press, 1948), pp. 8, 307.
16. Ibid., p. 70.
17. Ibid., p. 306.
18. Ibid., p. 76.
19. Ibid., p. 309.
20. Ibid., p. 314.
21. Ibid., pp. 310, 26.
22. *The Liberal Tradition in America: An Interpretation of American Political Thought Since the Revolution* (New York: Harcourt, Brace and Co., 1955), p. 111.
23. Ibid., pp. 127–28.
24. Ibid., p. 63.
25. Ibid.
26. Ibid., p. 285.
27. Ibid., p. 248.
28. Ibid., p. 286.
29. Ibid., p. 287.
30. Ibid., pp. 153, 172.
31. Ibid., pp. 74, 89.
32. Ibid., p. 43.
33. "South Carolina Versus the United States," in *America*

*in Crisis*, ed. Daniel Aaron (New York: Alfred A. Knopf, 1952), pp. 80, 82, 83.

34. "Democracy: Image and Reality," in *Power and Civilization: Political Thought in the Twentieth Century*, ed. David Cooperman and E. V. Walter (New York: Thomas Y. Crowell Co., 1962), pp. 375, 378–85.

35. "The Rise of the Democratic Idea," in *Paths of American Thought*, ed. Arthur M. Schlesinger, Jr., and Morton White (Boston: Houghton Mifflin Co., 1963), p. 41.

36. Ibid., pp. 45, 43.

37. Ibid., p. 49.

38. *The Founding of New Societies* (New York: Harcourt, Brace and World, 1964), p. 11.

39. Ibid., pp. 91–92, 109.

40. Ibid., pp. 75–76.

41. Ibid., p. 87.

42. "The Rise of the Democratic Idea," p. 386.

43. *The Founding of New Societies*, pp. 24, 26.

44. *The Liberal Tradition in America*, p. 17.

45. "American Historiography and Comparative Analysis: Further Reflections," *Comparative Studies in Society and History* 5 (July, 1963): 368, 372.

# CHAPTER 4

## *DANIEL J. BOORSTIN AND THE SEARCH FOR COMMUNITY*

Daniel J. Boorstin has been the analyst of the social and political environment in which the American liberal thinks—the architect of the liberal's intellectual landscape. The most notable feature of this landscape has been Boorstin's concept of the community, which has been designed to provide for the liberal a haven from the terrors of ideological politics and for liberalism, a source of stability. This community, however, has come to preclude both reason and morality,[1] those factors which the Progressives considered the source of change and which, in the McCarthy era, came to be identified with ideological politics.

In building this community, Boorstin has drawn upon two interrelated strains of thought which emerged in the early 1950's: the "new conservatism," a theoretical rationale for the blending of conservative and liberal thought, and "pluralism," an empirical justification for an elitist democratic theory. The new conservatism had its basis in the lessened political differences between the two major political parties and the continuity between the Truman and Eisenhower administrations in the fifties. Although Eisenhower's dislike for the expanded role of the federal government and his appointment of prominent businessmen to his Cabinet indicated his own preference for free enterprise, he was unable to reverse the New Deal and Fair Deal trend toward the welfare state. Regulated capitalism, moreover, behaved benevolently, creating prosperity for the growing American middle class. The bipartisan support for foreign policy which had begun during World War II continued during Eisenhower's first term. He utilized the policy of containment to end the limited conflict in Korea, and Secretary of State John Foster Dulles' support for the formation of the Southeast Asia Treaty Organization to bolster the earlier NATO agreement indicated a continuation of international involvement. The Cold War threat had increased, however, with the fall of Nationalist China and the Russian explosion of the atomic bomb in 1949; with the American way of life seemingly at stake, liberals and conservatives found they had less to quarrel about and more to be mutually thankful for. This attitude was illustrated in 1952 by a *Partisan Review* symposium on "Our Country and Culture,"[2] in which most of the respondents agreed that "many writers and intellectuals now feel closer to their country and culture."[3] They gave as reasons the threat of Communism, a lessening sense of cultural inferiority to Europe, and the widening acceptance of art and the intellect in the United States. The Cold War climate was revealed in the response of one-time Marxist Sidney Hook, who explained his embracement of the American status quo by citing the "total threat which Communism poses to the life of the free mind."[4]

Underlying the frequent mention of their fears of Communism by exponents and practitioners of the new conservatism, however, was that increasing dissatisfaction voiced earlier by liberals with the Progressive optimistic view of man. The more dangerous the doctrines of Communist perfectionism appeared, the more deluded and misguided appeared the Progressive notion that man could perfect himself and his society. Daniel Aaron, for example, explained that the mood of the fifties grew out of a "profound mistrust not only for the theory and practice of Stalinism, but also for the progressive mind itself." The "current tragic view of history," he continued, and the "conception of the destructive and irrational impulses in men seemed to correspond more truthfully to the experience of this generation than the forecasts of the rational optimists."[5] The chief function of the new conservativism, said Clinton Rossiter, one of its able defenders and critics, was to "counter the optimism of the liberal and radical with certain cheerless reminders . . . : that evils exist independently of social or economic maladjustments; that we must search for the source of our discontents in defective human nature."[6] The similarity with postwar liberalism's view of human nature, as expressed by Schlesinger and Hartz, is obvious.

Man, according to this new doctrine, was imperfectly rational, inherently unequal, and of doubtful perfectibility. His greatest need was for a stable society, for large-scale social or political change created great anxiety. Of prime importance in such a society were property, a significant stabilizing force, and a multiplicity of groups and institutions to counter man's isolation.[7] In this context, Rossiter said, "abstract speculation, especially speculation aimed at ancient ways and natural urges," was a "major threat to stability."[8] The new conservatism, therefore, was simply the old liberalism refurbished in order to deny the definitive political theory that liberals had formerly asked for. With the ideologies of capitalism and perfectionism temporarily quelled, no liberal philosophy was necessary.

The new conservatives, however, were whistling in the dark, for even as they defended the New Deal status quo, Joseph McCarthy was attacking those accomplished liberal realities, the welfare state and the containment policy. Using the traditional arguments about economic individualism, McCarthy claimed that the New Deal was the work of Communists in high places, equating liberals with the perfectionist ideology. The Senate and two Presidents sat back, apparently helpless, as McCarthy demonstrated the power of a popularly elected leader to challenge the United States Army, to significantly shape the course of foreign policy, to destroy his political foes, like Millard E. Tydings, and to besmirch the names of responsible and loyal Americans like John Marshall. McCarthy's manipulation of the popular fear of Communism to usurp political power and stifle dissent re-aroused liberal fears of fascism.

So while the new conservatives praised the nonideological temper of the American populace, the pluralists[9] attempted to explain the ideological terrors of McCarthyism. These historians, political scientists, and sociologists were the mirror image of the new conservatives, liberals with conservative assumptions—a pessimistic view of human nature, a belief in the necessity for a stable society and in man's need for group membership to remedy his inherent inadequacies. These social scientists linked McCarthyism with both the reform methods and the goals of Progressivism. According to pluralist theory, the New Deal, through the leveling effects of its economic reforms, had created a mass society in which its citizens, the isolated and anxiety-ridden members of a "lonely crowd," readily succumbed to totalitarian movements such as McCarthy's.[10] Empirical studies seemed to substantiate this relationship between social isolation and mass political behavior. Seymour Martin Lipset, for example, found that those on the social periphery were likely to be intolerant, authoritarian, and indifferent to civil liberties,[11] a conclusion that was meant to apply not only to European fascism and Communism but to McCarthyism as well. Out of this empirical work came an elitist theory of democracy, which held that it was the small number of well-off, well-educated, and well-placed who participated in the democratic process and that widespread political participation was not only unnecessary but undesirable.[12] This redefined democratic theory was a clear and explicit rejection of the Progressive goal of a participatory democracy, which now seemed tied with European ideological politics.

The liberals themselves, however, had furnished McCarthy with his most powerful weapon, anti-Communism; his "evidence" of treason and disloyalty was drawn from Truman's own investigations of government employees. More important, McCarthy, describing his witch-hunting as a crusade against the Antichrist and a battle between good and evil, called for a moral revival and the return of moral values to politics,[13] as liberals themselves had done in the late forties. To McCarthy and his supporters, the containment policy did not produce clear-cut victories, because it did not rest on clear-cut moral and intellectual guidelines—again a reiteration of liberals' own criticisms of foreign policy in the earlier period. In the most significant pluralist analysis of McCarthyism, *The New American Right* (1955), editor Daniel Bell contended that McCarthyism represented "the tendency to convert issues into ideologies, to invest them with moral color and high emotional charge."[14] The liberals themselves had done the same, however, and the "intense ideological fanaticism"[15] of McCarthy sounded much like their own.

The pluralist response to McCarthy's dismaying usurpation of liberal arguments was still another attempt to divest liberalism and democracy of their perfectionist tendencies. "Democratic politics is bargaining and consensus because the historic contribution of liberalism has been to separate law from morality," Bell now concluded.[16] The other contributors concurred that the democratic norm was the pragmatic compromise of "interest politics, the clash of material aims and needs among various groups and blocs."[17] The proper concern of liberal politics was "relative standards of social virtue and political justice instead of abstract absolutes,"[18] as Bell later restated the proposition. In 1960, he proclaimed the "end of ideology" and the "exhaustion of political ideas,"[19] the latter being the pluralist equivalent of the new conservatism's rejection of political theory. Although Bell referred specifically to the triumph of the welfare state over the Marxist ideology of perfectionism, the "end" also symbolized the defeat of the Progressive belief that man as a rational and moral creature could reform his society.

This is the end at which Boorstin's community ultimately arrives. This community rested upon the analysis of American society by Alexis de Tocqueville,[20] who shared with the pluralists and the new conservatives the belief that the ideology of perfectionism springs from man's isolation and loneliness. Tocqueville did not use the term "ideology," which postdates his work; his equivalents were "abstractions," "universals," or "general ideas."

Tocqueville believed that there are two kinds of ideas: those which grow out of social and political experience and those which spring from social or political isolation. He had no use for the latter in the political arena, as he showed in *The Old Regime and the French Revolution*. The impetus for the Revolution, Tocqueville argued in this book, came from the "philosophers," whose "very way of living led [them] to indulge in abstract theories and generalizations regarding the nature of government. . . . For living as they did, quite out of touch with practical politics, they lacked the experience which might have tempered their enthusiasm." Therefore, the Revolution "was conducted in precisely the same spirit as that which gave rise to so many books expounding theories of government in the abstract. . . . The result was nothing short of disastrous."[21]

Tocqueville was undecided about what kind of ideas a democratic society produced. He frequently emphasized the practical nature of American thought.[22] Yet he also found that both democracy and equality in a nation "born free" created that isolation which produced abstractions. Democracy "throws [man] back forever upon himself alone and threatens in the end to confine him entirely within the solitude of his own heart."[23] Hence, "[m]en living in democratic countries . . . are apt to entertain unsettled ideas. . . . An abstract term is like a box with a false bottom; you may put in it what ideas you please and take them out again without being observed."[24] Equality has a similar effect: "In the ages of equality all men are independent of each other, isolated, and weak. . . . In order, therefore, to explain what is passing in the world, man is driven to seek for . . . great causes. . . . This again naturally leads the human mind to conceive general ideas and super-induces a taste for them."[25]

Tocqueville saw within the American political system and American society a number of factors which might prevent isolation, abstractions, revolution, and instability: "the democratic institutions which compel every citizen to take a practical part in the government moderate that excessive taste for general theories in politics which the principle of equality suggests."[26] Among these institutions, the most significant was the British system of local government: "the township," Tocqueville wrote, "seems to have come directly from the hand of God." He feared, however, that the local government he so admired would not survive in the face of the increasing political sophistication of the country.[27]

More reassuring were those institutions which dealt with the real heart of the problem, social equality, for Tocqueville maintained that the multiplicity of American associations cured the individual of the loneliness and atomization attendant upon equality. Such associations "remind every citizen, and in a thousand ways, that he lives in society." Therefore, "if men are to remain civilized or to become so, the art of associating together must grow and improve in the same ratio in which the equality of conditions is increased."[28]

Most important in countering isolation, however, was the principle of "self-interest rightly understood."[29] This principle, Tocqueville argued, was the last stronghold against the revolutionary potentials of political democracy and social instability, because self-interest provided the cement which held together the widely disparate and otherwise isolated American citizenry and engendered a "lasting" and "fruitful" form of patriotism.[30] Self-interest, moreover, concerned itself solely with the practical rather than with the theoretical aspects of life. It was, therefore, not only particularly appropriate to America, with its material abundance and its commercial spirit, but was a strong deterrent to political upheaval: first, because the striving for commercial gain diverts men from political agitation, and, second, because the practical love of property lessens the probability of revolution.[31]

Although Boorstin's concept of the stable community was to be built upon these counterforces to isolation—British institutions, American associations, and self-interest—*The Mysterious Science of the Law* (1941) was a critical examination of the institution of British common law, which Boorstin felt had bequeathed to the American legal system a reverence for unregulated private property evident, for example, in the conservative Supreme Court decisions during the New Deal. The book is an analysis of Sir William Blackstone's *Commentaries* and traces the intellectual process by which Blackstone justified the existing legal institutions. Boorstin found that Blackstone dealt, as does "every social scientist," with three elements: " 'Nature,' or the materials of experience, . . . ratiocination, or the process of 'Reason.' And finally, 'Values,' or the moral beliefs which the writer accepts."[32] Neither reason nor nature by itself provided a sound intellectual basis for the common law, Blackstone discovered. He was well aware of the destructive power of reason, and, Boorstin noted, "the French Revolution was to show where men might go when they were led by 'proud Reason' alone."[33] Yet nature alone also had socially disruptive implications, for the law of nature had been used by Locke to justify the English revolution of the seventeenth century and was to be used in the defense of later revolutions by Rousseau, Paine, Jefferson, and even Marx.[34] Blackstone, therefore, balanced reason with nature, or the Lockean concept of experience as the source of knowledge, thus creating a sort of philosophical equilibrium upon which the common law might rest.

This uneasy combination of reason and nature was given coherence and unity by Blackstone's values—life, liberty, and especially property, which occupied the "high altar of Blackstone's legal theology" and to which the other values were subordinate.[35] Although implicitly critical of the later liberal use of Blackstone's notion of the sanctity of private property, Boorstin maintained that Blackstone himself was not culpable for defending his values. "Indeed, I might say," Boorstin concluded, "that any student of society who felt profoundly the importance of certain values, and yet failed to enlist his critical faculties in support of those values, would be failing in his duty as a reasonable creature and a moral man." The *Commentaries*, therefore, should be judged not as a rational system but as a defense of one man's beliefs, for the function of man's reason was simply to "subserve some moral end."[36] *The Mysterious Science of the Law*, therefore, like Schlesinger's *Age of Jackson* and Hartz' *Economic Policy and Democratic Thought*, implied that intellectual abstractions were rightfully subordinate to economic realities; as in these books too, Boorstin's suggestion that the ends which man sought were more important than the means by which he sought them defended a pragmatism which discounted formal or reasoned philosophy in favor of the defense of moral values threatened in the prewar years by the possible victory of fascism over the Western democracies.

In 1948, however, *The Lost World of Thomas Jefferson* attacked pragmatism, which Boorstin now feared undermined moral values precisely because it had made unnecessary such a formal philosophy. Like *The Vital Center* and *The Liberal Tradition, The Lost World* was a call for a clearly articulated and more realistic liberal creed. For Boorstin too found within liberal pragmatism the source of both the postwar reversion to the ideology of laissez-faire and economic individualism and liberalism's susceptibility to the perfectionist ideology embodied in the Progressive party.

The purpose of *The Lost World,* Boorstin said, was to discover "the perils of the way of thought we have inherited from the Jeffersonians and hence [to] strengthen the philosophical foundations of a moral society in our day."[37] This "way of thought," growing out of the eighteenth-century struggle with nature, had obvious resemblances to pragmatism—its preference for action over theory and its use of the empirical evidence of nature or experience as the criterion of knowledge and truth. This pragmatic naturalism, Boorstin now found, had bequeathed an unfortunate legacy to later liberals. First, it subordinated human values to the material standards of nature; for example, it allowed the Jeffersonians to continue to entertain their belief in Negro inferiority despite their doctrine of universal equality, because they found no empirical evidence to the contrary.[38] Second, their belief that the individual inherits "rights" from nature permitted the Jeffersonians to neglect the interests of the community or the public welfare, and left the "moral ends" of government undefined.[39] In the nineteenth century, therefore, this concept of natural rights was used by Social Darwinists to justify men's struggles with each other for their individual aggrandizement,[40] a reference to the persistence of the laissez-faire ideology.

On the other hand, the overoptimism of pragmatism could be held responsible for the dissolution of the New Deal coalition, for the Jeffersonian "antipathy to speculative thought" encouraged later liberals to think that they did not need a philosophy. As a result, Boorstin warned, they ran the risk of succumbing to "inarticulate and unknown philosophies" or following "leaders who take [them] toward unknown and unknowable destinations."[41] The character of these "unknowable destinations" was made explicit by Boorstin's final comparison between eighteenth-century liberals and those who followed them. Jeffersonian thought, he said, was not utopian, for it knew "the incompleteness and imperfection of its practical accomplishments."[42] However, those who inherited its pragmatic temper and its proclivity for measuring man's capabilities by his mastery of nature, having seen that man had mastered nature in the nineteenth century, had come to believe that he could single-handedly shape his own destiny. Boorstin singled out three leading exponents of pragmatism who had helped to lay the foundations for Progressive thought—William James, John Dewey, and George Herbert Mead—as examples of "man [arrogating] to himself the energy, craftsmanship, and power of his Creator."[43] He accused these men, in short, of passing on to the liberals of his own day the ideology of perfectionism.

In these two early books, Boorstin had found inadequate two of the three elements with which he had said a social scientist must deal: reason, as embodied in the "science" of the common law, and nature, as expressed in Jeffersonian thought. Neither element alone provided a satisfactory basis for an enduring liberalism. Boorstin's liberal community, therefore, was to be modeled after Blackstone's philosophy, a stable compound of reason with nature, resting on moral values; this was Boorstin's version of the balance between idealism and realism sought by both Hartz and Schlesinger.

The subsequent challenges of ideological politics, however, cost Boorstin his faith, first, in reason, then in the moral values upon which his community was to rest, and, last, in nature itself. In 1950 and 1951 Boorstin rejected his earlier plea for a reasoned liberal creed, which he now believed, as did the new conservatives, would heighten Cold War tensions. For example, in a discussion of the American Revolution, Boorstin argued that the colonists were defending institutions, institutions which combined the rationalism of the common law and the naturalism of Jeffersonian thought.[44] Their defense, moreover, was "rooted in their habits and values."[45] The primary virtue of these institutions was that they made political theory unnecessary.[46]

*The Genius of American Politics* (1953) revealed that Boorstin now identified his earlier demand for a liberal theory with ideology: "the tendency to abstract the principles of political life" was equated with "the characteristic tyrannies of our age—naziism, facism, communism," all of which shared the assumption that "man can better his condition by trying to remake his institutions in some colossal image."[47] The "un-American demand for a philosophy of democracy"[48] with which to do battle against Communism indicated that liberals had fallen victim to European perfectionism, as McCarthy had shown.

Americans, Boorstin now claimed, have historically been institution-builders, not theoreticians. Their penchant for philosophy has been curbed by the fact of American community life. Boorstin's premise here, shared by Tocqueville as well as by the new conservatives and the pluralists, was that philosophy or theory is produced only by men living in isolation, who are also prone to totalitarianism. Boorstin pointed out, for example, that the Puritans had abandoned

their European thought system in the New World because
"the first establishment of a community in New England
was marked by . . . a decline in man of the fears and uncer-
tainties which had nourished [this] desperate dependence
on God."[49]

More important, McCarthy's perversion of liberal pleas
that democracy wage a moral battle against Communism
led Boorstin, like the pluralists, to remove from his community the moral values upon which it had earlier rested, because they created disastrous division and internal conflict,
and thus threatened social stability. The American Revolution and the Civil War, Boorstin now concluded, were moderate because they "tended to side-step the moral issue." Only
Americans like the abolitionists insisted upon being "absolutist and abstract"; they, significantly, "kept the fires of controversy burning." Such utopianism has never been typical of
American thought, which has been a "unique combination
of empiricism and idealism."[50]

Boorstin's next book, *The Americans: The Colonial Experience* (1958), the first volume of a proposed trilogy, indicates
the importance of the removal of both moral abstractions
and political theory from his community. The title itself reveals Boorstin's reversion to naturalism, for the book describes the adaptation of the American settlers to nature,
which Boorstin had defined in *The Mysterious Science* as
"the materials of experience." Although there was here too
the description of the Puritans as community-builders "more
interested in institutions that functioned than in generalities
which glittered,"[51] Boorstin had begun to have doubts about
the stability of American political institutions seemingly
threatened by McCarthyism, describing them in 1956 as
"tenuous and . . . elusive."[52] He then fell back on the factor
which ultimately stabilized Tocqueville's America and
Blackstone's philosophy: property and man's self-interest.

Predictably, Boorstin, like Hartz, found that economics rather than moral issues were the legitimate concerns of democratic politics. The democratic norm was the Virginia House of Burgesses, in which there was a "wholesome identification of self-interest with political activity." Virginia, Boorstin said, was governed by propertied "men of affairs rather than . . . visionaries, reformers, or revolutionaries";[53] their political criteria were not the abstractions of moral values or theory but self-interest.

Boorstin's second volume, *The Americans: The National Experience* (1965), also described the America of the early national period in terms of the adaptation of Americans to their natural environment: their towns, their leaders, and their talk. There was again the pluralist emphasis on men as members of groups and communities, and the implications of Boorstin's concept of community were made clear: "A by-product of looking for ways of living together was a new civilization, whose strength was less an idealism than a willingness to be satisfied with less than the ideal." A community, Boorstin said, also provided the best setting for the expression of self-interest, for "communities were expressly created to serve private interests, and private interests were preserved only by the express construction of effective communities."[54] The inhabitant of this nineteenth-century community was the American businessman, Boorstin's version of Horatio Alger, whose "starting belief was in the interfusing of public and private prosperity." He was, moreover, "an American institution," whose "career and ideals are an allegory of an American idea of community."[55]

The concept of community has continued to be central to Boorstin's thought. Threatened in the 1960's, however, by the increasing tendency of Americans to become utopian, by greater contact with European ideologies, and by "a direct democracy of public relations" which created a continually

politicized American electorate,[56] Boorstin's community did
not survive in its simple nineteenth-century form. In what
appeared to be merely a bad pun, Boorstin proposed in 1967
his idea of the "consumption community," by which he
meant a group of people held together by their preference
for Doublemint chewing gum. Such a community was
"quick," "non-ideological," and based on "the great American
democracy of cash." He then pinpointed the one factor
which would stabilize his community: "the material goods
that historically have separated men from one another, have
become, under American conditions, symbols which hold
men together."[57]

The search for community began at least as early as the
political theories of Plato and Aristotle. With its claim for a
higher moral value for the social or political order than for
the individual, communitarianism has run counter to the individualism of traditional liberal thought. And as Boorstin
originally conceived it in *The Lost World*, the community
was intended as a weapon against the liberal ideology of economic individualism, injurious to the higher moral claims of
the public welfare. Boorstin here followed the lead of two
Progressive social scientists, Dewey and Mead, both of
whom had maintained that man developed his fullest individuality only in association with others.[58] Yet, although
Boorstin initially shared their goals, in 1948 he had specifically labeled as utopian their view that man could change
his institutions through reason. Boorstin's own community,
therefore, was intended to offset the reality of man's self-
interestedness with the idealism of public welfare—or in
other words, to balance nature with reason.

When it appeared, however, that the belief in reason, associated with a perfectionist political philosophy, threatened
this community, its goal became not the self-development of
man but simply the prevention of that isolation which leads

to ideology and chaos. The removal of reason also led to Boorstin's reversion to naturalism, which, as he himself pointed out in *The Lost World*, made moral values irrelevant and unnecessary. In the state of nature Boorstin then created, the only value was property. And in this kind of community, political democracy became transformed into an elitist economic process guided by the self-interested businessman. Boorstin had, therefore, removed not only ideology from his community, but democracy and equality as well, the dangers of which Tocqueville had described.

In the late sixties, however, Boorstin found that even this community was endangered, not only by the men of reason and morality but by the "new barbarians," the student and black-power groups. Unlike traditional radicalism, Boorstin argued, these movements denied the community in their selfish drive for power. Most significantly, they represented the "social expression of a movement from Experience to Sensation."[59] Yet within Boorstin's own terms, these young people only displayed in exaggerated form the characteristics which he originally considered virtues, for like him, they repudiated reason in favor of nature—the difference between "Experience," or nature, and "Sensation" being a tenuous and primarily semantic one. This generation, appropriately enough, is both the literal and the symbolic offspring of Boorstin's businessman and illustrates the revolutionary potentials of their father's selfishness.

Without moral values, the foundation on which Blackstone's equilibrium between reason and nature depends, Boorstin's community is inherently unstable and potentially chaotic. In it dwell only institutions, and perhaps that lonely liberal Boorstin himself, in the splendid isolation he has tried so hard to prevent.

## NOTES

1. For the anti-intellectualism inherent in Boorstin's work, see John Higham, "The Cult of the 'American Consensus': Homogenizing American History," *Commentary* 27 (February, 1959): 93–100; Bernard Bailyn, "History and the Distrust of Knowledge," *New Republic* 139 (December 15, 1958): 18. On Boorstin's ethical relativism, see John P. Diggins, "The Perils of Naturalism: Some Reflections on Daniel J. Boorstin's Approach to American History," *American Quarterly* 23 (May, 1971): 162, 177.

2. *Partisan Review* 19 (May–June, 1952): 282–327; (July–August, 1952): 420–50; (September–October, 1952): 562–97.

3. Ibid., pp. 282–84.

4. Ibid., p. 569.

5. "Conservatism, Old and New," *American Quarterly* 6 (Summer, 1954): 99–100.

6. *Conservatism in America* (New York: Alfred A. Knopf, 1956), p. 21.

7. For statements of the conservative position, see Clinton Rossiter, *Conservatism in America*; Russell Kirk, *The Conservative Mind from Burke to Santayana* (Chicago: Henry Regnery Co., 1953); or Peter Viereck, "Liberals and Conservatives, 1789–1951," *Antioch Review* 11 (December, 1951): 387–96.

8. *Conservatism in America*, p. 52.

9. The term is used by Michael Paul Rogin in *The Intellectuals and McCarthy: The Radical Spectre* (Cambridge, Mass., and London: M.I.T Press, 1967), pp. 10–19 and passim, to refer to that group of historians and political sociologists who linked McCarthyism and Populism: Richard Hofstadter, Seymour Martin Lipset, Talcott Parsons, Edward Shils, David Riesman, Nathan Glazer, Oscar Handlin, Peter Viereck, Will Herberg, Daniel Bell, and William Kornhauser.

10. Good illustrations of mass theorists who link social iso-

lation with susceptibility to totalitarianism are Eric Hoffer, *The True Believer* (New York: Mentor Books, 1958), and William Kornhauser, *The Politics of a Mass Society* (Glencoe, Ill.: Free Press, 1963), esp. pp. 16, 108–10.

11. *Political Man: The Social Bases of Politics* (Garden City, N.Y.: Anchor Books, 1963), pp. 87–126.

12. Ibid., pp. 183–226; see also Lester W. Milbrath, *Political Participation: How and Why Do People Get Involved in Politics?* (Chicago: Rand McNally and Co., 1966), p. 153.

13. Michael Paul Rogin, *The Intellectuals and McCarthy*, pp. 32–58, notes the animus of pluralists to moral values in politics but relates this to their hostility to Populism rather than to Progressivism or the liberals' own earlier position.

14. Daniel Bell, "Interpretations of American Politics," in *The Radical Right*, ed. Daniel Bell (Garden City, N.Y.: Anchor Books, 1964), p. 71. This is an expanded and updated version of *The New American Right*, ed. Daniel Bell (New York: Criterion Books, Inc., 1955).

15. Ibid., p. 64.

16. Ibid., pp. 70–71.

17. Richard Hofstadter, "The Pseudo-Conservative Revolt," in *The Radical Right*, p. 64.

18. *The End of Ideology: On the Exhaustion of Political Ideas in the Fifties* (Glencoe, Ill.: Free Press, 1960), p. 276.

19. Ibid.

20. John Higham in *History* (Englewood Cliffs, N.J.: Prentice-Hall, 1965), pp. 221–22, comments on Tocqueville's postwar revival among historians. Even earlier, however, sociologists and political scientists were taken with Tocqueville's predictions about American mass society; see, for example, J. P. Mayer, *Alexis de Tocqueville: A Biographical Essay in Political Science*, trans. M. M. Boxman and C. Hahn (New York: Viking Press, 1940), esp. p. xvii.

21. Alexis de Tocqueville, *The Old Regime and the French Revolution*, trans. Stuart Gilbert (Garden City, N.Y.: Anchor Books, 1955), pp. 141, 147.

22. *Democracy in America*, trans. Phillips Bradley, 2 vols. (New York: Vintage Books, 1945), 2: 47.
23. Ibid., p. 106.
24. Ibid., p. 74.
25. Ibid., p. 17.
26. Ibid., p. 20.
27. *Democracy in America*, 1: 62.
28. *Democracy in America*, 2: 112, 118.
29. Ibid., p. 131.
30. Quoted in J. P. Mayer, *Alexis de Tocqueville*, pp. 37–38; *Democracy in America*, 1: 251.
31. Tocqueville, *Democracy in America*, 2: 268–70.
32. Daniel J. Boorstin, *The Mysterious Science of the Law* (Cambridge, Mass: Harvard University Press, 1941), p. 7.
33. Ibid., p. 19.
34. Ibid., p. 48.
35. Ibid., p. 166. The emphasis on property is also noted by David Noble, *Historians Against History: The Frontier Thesis and the National Covenant in American Historical Writing Since 1830* (Minneapolis: University of Minnesota Press, 1965), p. 160.
36. *The Mysterious Science*, pp. 188, 191.
37. *The Lost World of Thomas Jefferson* (Boston: Beacon Press, 1960), p. xii.
38. Ibid., pp. 49–54, 92.
39. Ibid., p. 195.
40. Ibid., p. 242.
41. Ibid., pp. 170–71.
42. Ibid., p. 239.
43. Ibid., pp. 247–48.
44. Review of *The Papers of Thomas Jefferson*, ed. Julian P. Boyd, vol. 1, in *William and Mary Quarterly* 7 (October, 1950): 595–609; vol. 2, in *William and Mary Quarterly* 8 (April, 1951): 283–85.
45. Ibid., vol. 1, p. 600.
46. Ibid., p. 608.
47. *The Genius of American Politics* (Chicago: University of Chicago Press, 1953), pp. 3, 7.

48. Ibid., p. 185.
49. Ibid., p. 53.
50. Ibid., pp. 111, 16.
51. *The Americans: The Colonial Experience* (New York: Random House, 1958), p. 16.
52. Review of *The Papers of Thomas Jefferson*, ed. Boyd, vols. 4-6, in *William and Mary Quarterly* 13 (October, 1956): 572.
53. *The Colonial Experience*, p. 121.
54. *The Americans: The National Experience* (New York: Random House, 1965), pp. 1, 72.
55. Ibid., pp. 115-16.
56. *The Image, or What Happened to the American Dream* (New York: Atheneum, 1962), p. 241; *America and the Image of Europe: Reflections on American Thought* (Cleveland and New York: World Publishing Co., 1964), pp. 123, 116.
57. "Welcome to the Consumption Community," *Fortune* 76 (September 1, 1967): 118, 134, 138.
58. John Dewey, in *The Public and Its Problems* (Denver: Allan Swallow, n.d.), proposes a "Great Community" to replace the smaller communities or "publics" upon which democracy was originally based. Boorstin seems directly indebted to Mead, who emphasized the importance of institutions to man's social life and his self-development through language, as Boorstin did in *The Americans*; see George Herbert Mead, *Mind, Self, and Society from the Standpoint of a Social Behaviorist* (Chicago: University of Chicago Press, 1934).
59. "The New Barbarians," *Esquire* 70 (October, 1968): 162.

# CHAPTER 5

# EDMUND MORGAN AND
# THE SEARCH FOR PRINCIPLE

Edmund S. Morgan has approached the problem of the post-war liberal through his prototype, the intellectual; Morgan is the historian of *the* intellectuals in American politics, the Puritans and the leaders of the American Revolution. He is also perhaps the best example of the "counter-Progressive"[1] thrust of liberal history. *The Stamp Act Crisis* (1953), written with his wife, Helen M. Morgan, was intended to refute the Progressives' contention that the colonists shifted their objections to British imperial regulations with changes in economic circumstances;[2] Morgan argued that the colonists, to the contrary, were steadfast in their refusal to pay taxes of any kind without representation and thus were motivated not by self-interest or economic considerations but by unchanging principles. His *Birth of the Republic* (1956) interpreted the Revolution as a reluctant but principled break with the mother country that neither was intended to nor did in fact achieve significant political reforms, as the Progressives had claimed.[3] Like his Harvard professor Perry Miller, Morgan has revised the stereotype of the Puritans as bigoted reactionaries which Progressive historians like Vernon Parrington had created. Morgan's own sympathetic biographies of John Winthrop and Ezra Stiles have done much to humanize the Puritan image and provide insight into Puritan thought.

Morgan's second concern has been the reevaluation of the Progressive version of the political role of the intellectual or the man of reason as the bearer of moral values and the vehicle of change. Morgan has attempted to divest the intellectual of his perfectionist belief in man's rational and moral capabilities without relinquishing the intellectual's role as reformer. He has sought that "principle" by which the intellectual might reconcile the life of the mind with life in the political arena; Morgan refers to this as "the Puritan dilemma," the problem of being in but not of the world. His work illustrates the difficulties of this role for the intellectual, particularly as it was defined during the late 1950's.

The 1952 *Partisan Review* symposium had reflected confidence in the increasing rapport between the American public and the intellectual community made newly conservative by benevolent capitalism and malevolent Cold War Communism. This confidence, however, was overstated at the time and did not survive what intellectuals perceived as attacks upon themselves and the life of the mind. Intellectuals resented McCarthy's assault upon the reforms engineered by Roosevelt's "Brain Trust" and on the containment policy formulated by the scholar-diplomat George Kennan. Capitalizing upon the conviction for perjury of Alger Hiss, symbol of Eastern higher education to the American public, McCarthy charged that the treasonous activities of the State Department—the broken promises at Yalta and the fall of Chiang Kai-shek—could be laid at the doorstep of this academic elite; his accusations against the former Columbia University law professor Philip C. Jessup and Owen Lattimore, professor at Johns Hopkins University, likewise indicated his animus toward the intelligentsia. The investigation of the Voice of America by McCarthy's henchmen, David G. Schine and Roy M. Cohn, led to scattered incidents of book-burning, and intellectuals were frightened by the imposition of loyalty oaths in universities and by attacks on academic freedom.

The fate of Adlai Stevenson, the intellectuals' candidate by virtue of his wit and intelligence, was interpreted as a sign of popular hostility to the life of the mind. Labeled an "egghead" because he had attended Harvard Law School and deliberately smeared by McCarthy because he had been a character witness for Hiss, Stevenson was soundly defeated by the popular hero Eisenhower, who subsequently described an intellectual as "a man who takes more words than are necessary to say more than he knows."[4] However, although Stevenson remained a critic of the Eisenhower administrations, there was little difference between his policies and those of the President, for Stevenson was a chastened liberal of the new conservative variety. No foe of capitalism, Stevenson perpetuated the mild idealism of the New Deal era. His candidacies in 1952 and 1956 had been reluctant and marked by an aloofness from the general public suitable for a liberalism which had already repudiated a populistic democracy. Moreover, after McCarthy's censure by the Senate, with the strong albeit tardy backing of an administration which retained the essentials of the New Deal, liberals became reconciled to Eisenhower's moderate conservativism or conservative moderation.

What was still necessary, however, was an assessment of what had gone wrong between the intellectuals and the people in the first place. Much of this soul-searching went on in the growing body of literature which explained anti-intellectualism either as popular hostility to the intellectual's association with change or reform, or as the innate intolerance of democratic equalitarianism to the elitism of the intellect and superior education. Merle Curti, for example, in one of his attempts to mediate between the intellectuals and the larger public, offered two reasons for "the recent attacks by demagogues on intellectuals. . . . One is the challenge of totalitarianism in general and the 'cold war' in particular. The other

stretches back into our history much longer—the equalitarianism associated with democracy."[5] Seymour Martin Lipset
and David Riesman argued that anti-intellectualism was actually prompted by the elevation of intellectuals into a powerful elite, as in the New Deal Brain Trust, to which the mass
man was hostile.[6] The popular fear of the reform brought
about by this elite was a common theme in a series of articles in the *Journal of Social Issues* in 1955 that examined the
historical, psychological, and sociological origins of anti-
intellectualism.[7] In short, anti-intellectualism seemed to
spring from those very conditions of economic and political
equality which the intellectual, in his Progressive role as reformer, had helped to bring about; the intellectuals, as opponents of the ideology of laissez-faire capitalism during the
New Deal, had been all too successful. They had failed, however, to combat the ideology of perfectionism within their
own ranks. However unfounded McCarthy's charges of subversion and fellow-traveling were in the fifties, the uncom-
fortable fact remained that, as liberals well knew, much of
the intellectual community had been well to the left of center during the thirties.[8] Liberals had supported the alliance
with the Soviet Union during the war and had then reversed
themselves and clamored about those intellectuals who supported Wallace in 1948. McCarthy accused the liberals of
treason, much as liberals themselves had accused the Wallace
Progressives of betraying liberalism. Moreover, even while
liberals had chided those who succumbed to Wallace, they
had themselves, in the interests of anti-Communism, insisted
upon the necessity of moral values and philosophy in politics and had, therefore, fallen into the error of perfectionism.
McCarthy simply reminded the intelligentsia in a crude and
brutal way of those past sins which sprang from its inherent
susceptibility to the belief in man's capabilities. Again, the
Progressives seemed to blame, for they had defined the intel-

lectual as the conveyor of political morality and philosophy. McCarthy's evaluation of the intellectual was painfully correct.

In 1958 Edward Shils explicitly identified ideological politics with reason and morality and with the intellectual. Writing of "Italian Fascism, German National Socialism, Russian Bolshevism . . . and their fledgling American kinsman, McCarthyism," Shils said that ideological politics operated on the "assumption that politics should be conducted from the standpoint of a coherent, comprehensive set of beliefs" and rested upon "moral separatism." Intellectuals, he continued, were especially prone to this kind of politics because their traditions were generally hostile to established society and were infused with "sacred values."[9] Not very hopefully, Shils urged that intellectuals practice instead "civil politics," which, while not eschewing moral issues completely, would understand the "complexity of virtue, that no virtue stands alone, that virtues are intertwined with evils." "Is it too much to hope," he asked, that intellectuals "bring the age of ideology to an end?"[10]

Therefore, just as McCarthyism had indicated the need to redefine liberalism, McCarthy himself revealed an equally pressing need for a rethinking of the intellectual's relationship to the larger society and his role in public life. It was Daniel Bell who defined this new relationship as "alienation." By this he meant "a detachment, which guards against being submerged in any cause or accepting any particular embodiment of the community as final." Although critical of both "the utopian order and existing society," alienation did not entail "denial of one's roots and country."[11] Such a posture, Bell concluded, was "one of the safeguards for intellectuals, lest they become committed to the winds of ideology."[12] Alienation, therefore, neither affirmed nor denied the status quo and neither rejected nor accepted moral val-

ues in the political realm; it was the intellectual's own version of the familiar liberal equilibrium between realism
and idealism, a balance between the ideologies of economic
individualism and perfectionism. Although alienation indicated an ostensible reluctance to abandon the traditional
role of the intellectual as reformer, the attempt to play this
role was to be ultimately unsuccessful, for the balance would
collapse as it had in the definition of liberalism itself.

It is this balance which Morgan's "principle" is intended
to achieve. The dichotomy here is provided by Max Weber's
definition of inner- and other-worldliness. Weber's *The Protestant Ethic and the Spirit of Capitalism* described the dual
nature of Protestantism upon which Morgan has relied. The
thesis of the book was that there was an affinity between
Protestantism, especially Puritanism, and capitalism: "The
Puritan outlook . . . stood at the cradle of modern economic
man."[13] Central to this relationship, said Weber, was the
concept of the "calling," which taught that salvation must
be sought in this world. Hence, the monastic life formerly associated with religion was "not only quite devoid of value as
a means of justification before God" but was considered a
"renunciation of the duties of this world."[14] Of equal importance to the growth of capitalism was the rational, orderly
way in which life in this world had to be pursued. As a result, "active self-control . . . was the most important ideal of
Puritanism."[15] Weber called this rational pursuit of a "calling" in the world which fostered capitalism "inner-worldly
asceticism."

Protestantism had another side, however. This was Pietism,
which "wished to make the invisible Church of the elect
visible on this earth . . . and attempted to live . . . a life free
from all the temptations of the world." Pietism involved not
only a rejection of the world, or other-worldliness, but an
emotionalism which was "the direct opposite of the strict and
temperate discipline" of asceticism.[16]

The tension between these dual aspects of Protestantism meant that the Protestant must seek to live "a life in the world but neither of nor for this world."[17] Moreover, for Weber, the intellectual embodied in a curious way both inner- and other-worldliness. He was, on the one hand, identified with that rationalism associated with inner-worldliness. On the other hand, "the conflict of [his] requirement of meaningfulness with the empirical realities of the world and its institutions, and with the possibilities of conducting one's life in the empirical world, are responsible for the intellectual's characteristic flights from the world."[18]

Weber also found that inner- and other-worldliness had counterparts in the political realm. Politics, he said, can be oriented to an "ethic of ultimate ends" or to an "ethic of responsibility." The first alternative was associated with the other-worldly intellectual: "In the world of realities . . . we encounter the ever-renewed experience that the adherent of ultimate ends suddenly turns into a chiliastic prophet . . . [for he] cannot stand up under the ethical irrationality of the world."[19] Both ethics, Weber maintained, had risks:

> Everything that is striven for through political action operating with violent means and following an ethic of responsibility endangers the "salvation of the soul." If, however, one chases after the ultimate good in a war of beliefs, following a pure ethic of absolute ends, then the goals may be damaged and discredited for generations because responsibility for consequences is lacking.

What was necessary, then, was a "taming of the soul" through which the man with a "calling for politics" might combine the ethic of responsibility with the ethic of ultimate ends.[20]

Weber, then, laid the foundation for Morgan's "Puritan dilemma," that conflict between inner- and other-worldly de-

mands which Morgan described in his biography of John
Winthrop: "[T]he central problem of Puritanism has concerned every man of principle of every age, not least of all
our own. It was the question of what responsibility a righ-
teous man owes to society. If society follows a course he con-
siders morally wrong, should he withdraw and keep his principles intact, or should he stay?"[21] Like John Winthrop,
Morgan's intellectuals had to find that "principle" which
would guide them between an escapist search for other-
worldly perfectionism and an inner-worldly pursuit of capitalism.

Morgan first laid down this principle in *The Puritan Family* ( 1944 ), which described a pursuit of purity and perfection representing escapism. The book portrayed the Puritan
intellectuals as separatists who came to this country to "protect themselves and their children from the wicked world,"
hoping to "establish their ideal state without molestation."
Because they came "in order to preserve their faith, not to
extend it,"[22] the Puritans abandoned their responsibility to
save the world, as perhaps the Progressives had by their reluctance to have the United States enter World War II on
the Allied side. As Schlesinger had pointed out in *The Age
of Jackson*, the ideology of perfectionism also thwarted genuine reform, which dealt not with utopian schemes, but
with the harsh realities of this world.

McCarthy's crusade against the moral evil of Communism,
however, gave a new meaning to the ideology of perfectionism, which is revealed in Morgan's *The Stamp Act Crisis*.
Like *The Puritan Family*, this later book described an other-
worldly pursuit of the "ethic of absolute ends" in politics:
the clash between British "absolute authority" and colonial
"inalienable rights."[23] The ultimate outcome, of course, was
the Revolution and colonial independence, which Morgan
had to accept. What he deplored, however, were the immedi-

ate results of this "genuine and irreconcilable conflict"[24] which preceded the shooting war between the British and the colonists: mob rule, demagoguery, and violence, leading to incidents like the destruction of Lieutenant Governor Thomas Hutchinson's house by an angry crowd protesting the Stamp Act. Hutchinson's "fundamental conservatism" incurred the wrath of the populace, for he "thought it foolhardy for a people to seek a head-on collision with Parliament by abstract declarations of their rights."[25] He, therefore, suffered the fate of those few wiser and more responsible men who "tried to halt the approach of disaster. The results in every case were ruined lives."[26] Despite their conservatism, men like Hutchinson and Jared Ingersoll were tainted by their earlier association with the Stamp Act, the embodiment of British absolutism; they therefore learned the lessons that McCarthy later taught intellectuals such as Adlai Stevenson: "guilt by association, as more than one American has learned, cannot be washed away by a mere demonstration of innocence. . . . There might be many brave hearts that loved Mr. Ingersoll . . . but not enough to win an election."[27] Perfectionism here was not an obstacle to reform but a radical and destructive force; it was, moreover, an ideology to which the intellectual was particularly prone, as was shown in *The Puritan Family*, and one which brought down upon his head the wrath of the people.

As Shils had argued, what was clearly needed was a restating of that "principle" which would divorce the intellectual from this brand of ideology. Morgan had concluded in 1953 that "the significance of the Stamp Act crisis lies in the emergence of [the] well-defined constitutional principles" over which the Revolution was fought,[28] and in *The Birth of the Republic* (1956) Morgan declared that the Revolution itself was a "search for principles."[29] He found that there were three principles at issue: liberty, equality, and nationalism.

Since he also found, however, that equality and nationalism were less causes than by-products of the Revolution, he concluded that it was the principle of liberty, springing from a "widespread ownership of property,"[30] that motivated and united the colonists. Although this concept of liberty involved the "coupling of principle and self-interest," Morgan argued that we must "remember that constitutional principles have been created and continue to exist for the protection of the people who live under them."[31] There were selfish interests involved in the writing of the Constitution too, he admitted, but "contrary to the impression given by [Charles] Beard, it is all but impossible to differentiate private selfishness from public spirit."[32] Guided by principle tempered by self-interest, therefore, the intellectual leaders of the Revolution could achieve the desirable balance between the other-worldly pursuit of liberty and the worldly pursuit of property. This was, then, Morgan's version of Bell's "alienation," a stance midway between acceptance and rejection of the world, a perilous balance between capitalism and perfectionism.

This principle, however, proved to be a hard one to live by, as Morgan showed in his treatment of John Winthrop in 1958. Through a "taming of the heart," Winthrop was at first able to solve "the problem of living in this world without taking his mind off God,"[33] thus successfully steering the middle course. But no sooner had he landed in the New World than the other-worldly separatist tendencies within Puritanism threatened the community. As governor, Winthrop found that "he must restrain the over-zealous from setting for the community a standard of godliness that would deny the humanity of human beings. He had learned not to expect perfection in this world and to march in company with other sinners, for sin, though it must be punished, could not be stamped out." Winthrop, then, by accepting political responsibility, chose life in the world, believing that "there was no escape from the dungheap of this earth; and that those who sought one or thought they had found it acted with an unholy, not a holy, violence."[34]

Having sought the liberal balance between realism and idealism, between inner- and other-worldly values, Morgan realized, earlier than Schlesinger, that the "vital center" would not hold and that the intellectual must choose between two alternatives. The meaning of this choice was revealed in 1962 in Morgan's portrait of Ezra Stiles. Stiles had emerged from a youthful struggle between reason and religious revelation with "a faith in the unrestricted use of reason, a faith that he blended with his faith in God."[35] Stiles believed that although human reason was imperfect, it was the only way of arriving at those proximate truths which man was capable of perceiving. He was therefore tolerant of the religious beliefs of others, unlike his less enlightened contemporaries who "failed to see that absolute certainty in theological matters was impossible of attainment."[36]

Early in his career Stiles had also been merely "a spectator rather than an active participant in the world around him. He could take as much interest in politics as he chose, but he must not influence them in any way. . . . He could believe in liberty, but he need not fight for it." Although this halfway stance spared him the agonies of political involvement, it was not easy, Stiles discovered, to "live close to his fellow men without participating in their worldly affairs";[37] for example, during the early years of the Revolution Stiles was attacked for his neutrality by both the Tories and the patriots. When Stiles accepted the presidency of Yale, however, he was forced, like Winthrop, to abandon the middle course and to enter "the turbulent secular world."[38] He thus faced anew the problem he had wrestled with for many years: how "to live the life of the mind and the spirit in a po-

litical and pragmatic world. . . . Ezra Stiles knew as well as
anyone that the intellectual in any country must keep much
to himself, for thought shrivels in public. But he knew that
the intellectual owes responsibilities to the world." Stiles
was, therefore, wiser than his fellow intellectuals of the period, who deserted their responsibilities and their congrega-
tions for the pleasures of the library and hence "opened
[the] breach" between intellectuals and the community
which still existed.[39]

Morgan's *Visible Saints* (1963) was another warning to the
escapist intellectual. The Puritan effort in the 1630's and
1640's to establish saving grace as a criterion for church
membership, Morgan argued, involved "the danger of de-
serting the world in search of a perfection that belongs only
to heaven" and represented the Puritans' neglect of their responsibilities to the larger community. The standards of perfection set by these zealots were ultimately unattainable, as
they discovered when their own children were barred from
their churches. The Puritans learned, as Winthrop and Stiles
had learned, that "the world has many ways of defeating
those who try to stand too far from it."[40]

Morgan further developed this theme in 1963 in "The
American Revolution Considered as an Intellectual Movement," which explained American anti-intellectualism—specifically, hostility to the clergymen of the pre-Revolutionary
period—as a not unjustified popular reaction to their absorp-
tion with abstract philosophical and theological questions
and their subsequent neglect of their followers. "The clergy,
once the most respected members of the community, became
the objects of ridicule and contempt."[41] By contrast, the new
intellectual leadership—Jefferson, Hamilton, Madison, and
Adams—dealt not with other-worldly abstractions, as Morgan
had argued in *The Stamp Act Crisis*, but with ideas which
corresponded to the realities of colonial life; they were par-

ticularly aware of the political necessity of a widespread distribution of property. Although their ascendancy was brief, these intellectuals thereby created "the most stable popular government ever invented."[42]

Morgan then reevaluated Roger Williams along these lines. In 1958 he had described Williams as "the soul of separatism."[43] He found in 1967, however, that "although Williams . . . was driven by a profound yearning for pure divinity, he would not allow himself to look beyond the world around him or through it."[44] Like the leaders of the Revolution, Williams was both a "man of action" and an intellectual;[45] he was consequently a political realist, who believed that government was the art of the possible, and a pragmatist, like Stiles, who defended religious toleration because he believed that there was no sure way to judge religious truth. Despite his reputation, then, Williams had no radical intentions, Morgan maintained. In fact, "those conservatives who today search the American past for intellectual ancestors to make them feel at home would with some plausibility lay claim to Williams."[46]

Morgan has, at this point, seemingly turned the Progressive interpretation of both the Puritans and the Revolutionaries completely around. Although, as he now argued, the primary thrust of Puritanism was radical in its drive for perfectionism, Roger Williams, construed by Parrington as a radical seventeenth-century democrat,[47] became a conservative. The Revolutionaries, motivated, according to the Progressives, by a desire for economic equality which would bring political democracy,[48] now merely sought economic equality in order to create political stability.

The transformation of these intellectuals was completed in "The Puritan Ethic and the American Revolution" (1967), which linked Morgan's two main interests, the Puritans and the Revolutionaries, with each other and with the American present. Morgan here argued that the principle behind the American Revolution was a secular version of the "Puritan ethic." The virtues associated with this ethic, industry and frugality, were at the heart of the argument against taxation without representation. This was

> a constitutional principle [which] was a means hallowed by history, of protecting property and of maintaining those virtues associated with property, without which no people could be free. Through the rhetoric of the Puritan ethic, the colonists reached behind the constitutional principles to the enduring human needs that brought the principle into being.

This ethic had in the past lessened sectional conflict and in the present provided the basis for our modern political parties, which have no "clear ideological differences" between them.[49] The "principle," then, is property, and the "enduring human need" is self-interest.

This conclusion indicates that Morgan's counter-Progressive thrust has been less than successful. Both *The Stamp Act Crisis* and *The Birth of the Republic* were attempts to overturn the Progressive economic interpretation of the colonial movement for independence. Elsewhere Morgan had criticized Beard's economic analysis of the Constitution because, he said, it devalued the "principles" of the Founding Fathers and "turned historians away from what men said to what they did, from politics to economics, . . . from the rational to the irrational and subconscious."[50] Morgan now suggested, however, that his own concept of the Puritan ethic might be the basis of "another economic interpretation of the Constitution."[51] This is the logical outcome of his analysis, for his "principle," by denying other-worldly perfectionism, comes ultimately to rest on inner-worldly capitalism, as did the liberal identity of Hartz and the community of Boorstin.

Nor did Morgan's redefinition of the Progressive role for the intellectual achieve the end which Morgan had initially desired. His earliest work was aimed at weaning the intellectual from his other-worldly pursuit of perfectionism, identified with Progressive thought, and recalling him to the realities of the world so that genuine reform might be accomplished. Morgan's brief attempt to achieve a balance between other-worldly idealism and inner-worldly realism in *The Birth of the Republic* was not successful. This "middle way" advocated by Schlesinger was the hardest to follow, for one was attacked by both the left and the right, as Ezra Stiles discovered. The man of reason, therefore, could fulfill his responsibilities only by living totally within the world.

Yet both "reason" and "the world" had come to have a particular meaning for Morgan. He frequently described the Puritans and the Revolutionaries as "rational" or "reasonable" men. However, his portraits of Stiles and Williams emphasized that, at best, reason is a fallible instrument by which man can arrive at only proximate truth. The most reliable source of knowledge, therefore, was experience or contact with material reality; the Revolutionaries, he found in 1966, were guided not by abstract theories or moral questions but by ideas which corresponded to the American realities of material abundance. It was in this sense of the term that Morgan described the colonists as "reasonable" when he was forced to explain why they continued to pay taxes on sugar and tea, having objected on "principle" to all British taxes; these men, Morgan said, "were prosperous. Reasonable men did not wish to tempt fate by demanding more or to meet conciliation with doctrinaire rigidity."[52] Reason,

then, is not the ability to bring about change, as it was for the
Progressives, but the ability to perceive economic realities
and one's own self-interest.

With reason so defined, the pursuit of perfection becomes
not only escapist but irrational. When Morgan's man of reason chose not to pursue the "ethic of absolute ends," the
moral principle was transformed into the material one, and
the man of principle became the man of property. Morgan's
intellectual, therefore, turned out to be Hartz' Horatio Alger
or Boorstin's businessman.

In 1944 living in the world meant for Morgan, as it did for
the Progressives, using one's reason to change it; if one did
not do so, he had not fulfilled his role as an intellectual. Since
1953, however, life in the world has meant something different. It has meant, for Morgan as it has for Schlesinger, facing the "facts" of human imperfection and seeing the self-
interest behind the principle, the desire for property behind
the desire for liberty. It has meant being a "reasonable"
man, one who is content with proximate truths and does not
tempt fate by asking for more than he already has or by
pressing his principles to extremes. Life in the world has
meant, as it finally did for Roger Williams, accepting the
world as it is—and thus being a conservative. Morgan has
asked his fellow intellectuals not to desert their worldly responsibilities, but what he has shown them is that "there is no
escape from the dungheap of this earth."[53]

## NOTES

1.  The term is borrowed from Gene Wise, *Explanation in Historical Studies: Some Strategies for Inquiry* (Homewood, Ill.: Dorsey Press, forthcoming).

2.  See, for example, Carl L. Becker, *The Declaration of Independence: A Study in the History of Political Ideas* (New York: Harcourt, Brace and Co., 1922).

3.  Becker, *The History of Political Parties in the Province of New York, 1760–1776* (Madison, Wis.: University of Wisconsin Press, 1909); J. Franklin Jameson, *The American Revolution Considered as a Social Movement* (Princeton: Princeton University Press, 1926); Arthur M. Schlesinger, *Colonial Merchants and the American Revolution* (New York: Columbia University Studies in History, Economics and Public Law, 1918).

4.  A good discussion of the anti-intellectual nature of McCarthyism, as well as a reflection of the liberal reaction to it, is to be found in Richard Hofstadter, *Anti-Intellectualism in American Life* (New York: Vintage Books, 1963), pp. 4–23.

5.  *American Paradox: The Conflict of Thought and Action* (New Brunswick, N.J.: Rutgers University Press, 1956), p. 65.

6.  Lipset, "American Intellectuals: Their Politics and Status," *Daedalus* 88 (Summer, 1959): 480–86; Riesman, "The Spread of Collegiate Values," in *The Intellectuals: A Controversial Portrait*, ed. George B. Huszar (Glencoe, Ill.: Free Press, 1960), pp. 505–9. See also "Comments on Lipset's 'American Intellectuals: Their Politics and Status,'" *Daedalus* 88: 487–98.

7.  Bernard Barber, "Sociological Aspects of Anti-Intellectualism," *Journal of Social Issues* 3 (1955): 25–30; William E. Leuchtenberg, "Anti-Intellectualism: An Historical Perspective," ibid., pp. 8–17; Rollo May, "A Psychological Approach to Anti-Intellectualism," ibid., pp. 41–47; S. Stanfield Sargent, "Introduction to Anti-Intellectualism in the United States," ibid., pp. 3–7.

8.  See, for example, Daniel Aaron, *Writers on the Left: Episodes in American Literary Communism* (New York: Harcourt, Brace and World, 1961), or Frank A. Warren III, *Liberals and Communism: The "Red Decade" Revisited* (Bloomington and London: Indiana University Press, 1966).

9.  Shils, "Ideology and Civility: On the Politics of the Intellectual," *Sewanee Review* 66 (July-September, 1958): 450, 452, 467.

10.  Ibid., pp. 472, 480.

11.  *The End of Ideology: On the Exhaustion of Political Ideas in the Fifties* (Glencoe, Ill.: Free Press, 1960), p. 16.

12.  "Comments on Lipset's 'American Intellectuals: Their Politics and Status,'" *Daedalus* 88 (Summer, 1959): 498.

13.  *The Protestant Ethic and the Spirit of Capitalism*, trans. Talcott Parsons (New York: Charles Scribner's Sons, 1959), p. 174.

14.  Ibid., p. 81.

15.  Ibid., p. 119.

16.  Ibid., p. 130.

17.  Ibid., p. 154.

18.  *The Sociology of Religion*, trans. Ephraim Fischoff (Boston: Beacon Press, 1963), pp. 124–25.

19.  "Politics as a Vocation," in *From Max Weber: Essays on Sociology*, ed. H. H. Gerth and C. Wright Mills (New York: Oxford University Press, 1958), pp. 120, 122.

20.  Ibid., pp. 126, 127.

21.  *The Puritan Dilemma: The Story of John Winthrop* (Boston and Toronto: Little, Brown and Co., 1958), p. xii.

22.  "Puritan Tribalism," *More Books*, 6th ser. 38 (May, 1943): 203–4. This article and another, "The Puritan Family and Social Order," *More Books*, 6th ser. 38 (January, 1943): 9–21, were chapters of *The Puritan Family: Religion and Domestic Relations in Seventeenth-Century New England* (Boston: Public Library, 1944).

23.  Edmund S. Morgan and Helen M. Morgan, *The Stamp*

*Act Crisis: Prologue to Revolution* (Chapel Hill: University of North Carolina, 1953), p. 1.

24. Ibid., p. 291.
25. Ibid., pp. 215, 219.
26. Ibid., p. 207.
27. Ibid., p. 237.
28. Ibid., p. 296.
29. *The Birth of the Republic* (Chicago: University of Chicago Press, 1956), p. 3.
30. Ibid., p. 7.
31. Ibid., pp. 51–52.
32. Ibid., p. 132.
33. *The Puritan Dilemma*, pp. 8–9.
34. Ibid., pp. 76, 130.
35. *The Gentle Puritan: A Life of Ezra Stiles* (New Haven and London: Yale University Press, 1962), p. 179.
36. Ibid., p. 447.
37. Ibid., pp. 245, 275.
38. Ibid., p. 310.
39. Ibid., p. 321.
40. *Visible Saints: The History of a Puritan Idea* (Ithaca, N.Y.: Cornell University Press, 1963), pp. 114, 112.
41. In *Paths of American Thought*, ed. Arthur M. Schlesinger, Jr., and Morton White (Boston: Houghton Mifflin Co., 1970), p. 22.
42. Ibid., p. 33.
43. *The Puritan Dilemma*, p. 116.
44. *Roger Williams: The Church and the State* (New York: Harcourt, Brace and World, 1967), p. 61.
45. Ibid., p. 4.
46. Ibid., pp. 125–26.
47. Vernon L. Parrington, *Main Currents in American Thought*, vol. 1, *The Colonial Mind: 1620–1800* (New York: Harcourt, Brace and World, 1954), pp. 62–75.
48. Becker, *The History of Political Parties in the Province of New York, 1760–1776*; Jameson, *The American Revolu-*

*tion Considered as a Social Movement*; Schlesinger, *Colonial Merchants and the American Revolution*.

49.  *William and Mary Quarterly*, 3rd ser. 24 (January, 1967): 14, 24. In a more recent article, however, "The Labor Problem in Jamestown, 1607–18," *American Historical Review* 75 (June, 1971): 595–611, Morgan appears to have reevaluated the prevalence of the Puritan ethic, for here he argues that the settlers in Jamestown were unwilling to work for a living and that the colony was an economic success only because they were able to enslave African blacks to do their work for them.

50.  "The Historians of Early New England," in *The Reinterpretation of Early American History*, ed. Ray Allen Billington (San Marino, Calif.: Huntington Library, 1966), p. 47.

51.  "The Puritan Ethic and the American Revolution," pp. 41–42.

52.  *The Birth of the Republic*, p. 53.

53.  *The Puritan Dilemma*, p. 130.

# CHAPTER 6

# *RICHARD HOFSTADTER AND*
# *THE END OF IDEOLOGY*

Richard Hofstadter is the most influential and the most persuasive of the liberal historians. An innovator in the field of psychohistory, with which he has exposed the quirks and foibles of American political thought and behavior, Hofstadter was likewise an early analyst of the liberal consensus in *The American Political Tradition* (1948) and a devastating critic of this tradition in *The Age of Reform* (1955). Regardless of method or content, however, Hofstadter has dealt explicitly or implicitly in all his work with the role of the intellectual in politics. His mission, like Morgan's, has been to divorce the intellectual from ideological politics and ultimately to bring about that "end of ideology" proclaimed by Daniel Bell. The "end" which Hofstadter has achieved, however, reveals the fate of the intellectual who is deprived of his role as moral critic and man of reason.

The "end of ideology," as Bell originally conceived it, was intended to define a stance for the intellectual which would make him invulnerable to the perfectionist ideology that led to the not unjustifiable popular hostility of the McCarthy era. The definition of this stance was not carried to its logical conclusion until the early sixties, however, when the administration of John F. Kennedy created an atmosphere again congenial to the intellectual community. The literature of the fifties had claimed that anti-intellectualism was inherent in a democratic society, but by 1957 the atmosphere had already changed when, in response to the Russian launching of Sputnik, the federal government began to grant aid to education under the National Defense Education Act. More important, Kennedy's election in 1960 was interpreted as a sign that intellectuals mattered again, at least to the people who mattered. Especially heartening was his victory over Richard Nixon, the bête noire of liberals because of his association with McCarthyism. Kennedy, a historian himself with two books to his credit, cultivated his image as an intellectual by making the White House a gathering place for representatives from the world of culture and by recruiting many of his personal and political staff members from the universities, particularly from his own alma mater, Harvard.

"The large-scale employment of intellectuals continues to be the most striking thing of all about the [Kennedy] administration," wrote Richard Rovere, waxing eloquent over the appointment of his colleague Schlesinger as White House Special Assistant. Rovere found an important reason, aside from Kennedy's personal tastes, for these appointments: "the expansion of government under the New Deal and in the years since has more or less required a steady increase in the use of experts that are nowadays found mainly in universities."[1] Rovere concluded on a somewhat cautious note about the political use of "men whose primary qualifications are their knowledge of problems, their understanding of theory, and their capacity for logical analysis. The great majority," he warned, "are new to power, and their education has included little in the way of training in the uses of power. It is a most radical experiment."[2]

Rovere's qualified optimism stemmed from the postwar redefinition of the legitimate concerns of liberalism as relative rather than absolute values and material gains rather than moral goals or philosophical questions. Given this definition, the political participation of the intellectual, with his proneness to the ideology of perfectionism, was indeed a "radical experiment." The Bay of Pigs disaster in April, 1961, did convince some observers that this experiment was a failure. Intellectuals are not equipped to handle foreign policy, said Hans Morgenthau, because they have no "sense of limits—limits of knowledge, of judgment, of successful action";[3] Alfred Kazin feared that Kennedy's reliance upon intellectuals might lead him to "identify the United States with a crusade, a cause, with 'liberty.' "[4]

As Rovere had implied, however, the use of the intellectual as "expert" was acceptable, for in this role he would focus his mind on concrete matters rather than on dangerous moral abstractions. Another commentator prophesied that since the needs of contemporary society could be met through rational planning rather than through class conflict, the intellectual would have a greater role in the systematized decision-making process.[5] One historian found the origins of this new function in the New Deal Brain Trust: "Roosevelt simply recognized," he explained, "that for many years higher education had been developing a strong utilitarian emphasis, and he gave that development a significant push forward by increasing the political opportunities of service intellectuals."[6]

This changed political context of the early sixties, then, provided the historical framework for Hofstadter's portrayal of the nonideological intellectual. The intellectual framework was furnished by Karl Mannheim's definition of "ideology" and its opposite, "utopia." The two types of thought systems, according to Mannheim, were distinguished not by their content but by their relationship to the status quo. Ideologies "direct activity toward the maintenance of the existing order"; utopias, on the other hand, "tend to generate activities toward changes of the prevailing order."[7] Mannheim held that ideas cannot be understood out of their social context, and, therefore, that ideologies were characteristic of "ruling groups," who "in their thinking become so intensely interest-bound to a situation that they are simply no longer able to see certain facts which would undermine their sense of dominance." Utopias, on the other hand, appeal to "oppressed groups," who are "intellectually so strongly interested in the destruction and transformation of a given condition of society that they unwittingly see only those elements in the situation which tend to negate it."[8] This was the aspect of Mannheim's thought which initially attracted Hofstadter: discussing the growth of his own interest in intellectual history, he wrote, "To me Mannheim provided the link I had been seeking between ideas and social situations."[9]

Ideas and social situations were linked by a belief which Mannheim shared with the Progressive pragmatists in the social or experiential basis of knowledge. This epistemology was particularly important in politics, where "it is precisely in the course of actual conduct that specific and relevant knowledge is attainable[10] and where, therefore, "purely theoretical contemplation" has no place.[11]

Despite the relativism of his epistemology, Mannheim nevertheless believed that man could attain some measure of objective truth. To this end, he proposed his "sociology of knowledge." Its purpose was to correct the false or partial truth of both ideologies and utopias by uncovering the "irrational foundations of rational knowledge";[12] it would thus free man's mind from those nonrational or social forces which shaped it. Intellectuals were to play a significant role in this process. Because they were an "unanchored, relatively classless stratum,"[13] they might be free of both the ideology of the ruling class and the utopia of the oppressed class. Mannheim hoped that intellectuals would create a synthesis of conflicting thought systems, acting as "advocate[s] of the intellectual interests of the whole" and "watchmen in what otherwise would be a pitch-black night."[14] Under special circumstances, however, intellectuals were to furnish utopias for societies in which they were lacking.[15] This is similar to the Progressive belief that the man of reason could transcend his immediate experience and furnish the society with goals and philosophies directed toward change.

Mannheim's aim of uncovering the irrational bases of man's thought and making it correspond to reality—of ending the ideology of capitalism and the utopia of Progressive perfectionism—has been shared by Hofstadter, who, like his colleagues, has found traditional liberalism incongruent with present facts. He has also found this ideological liberalism closely tied to the Protestantism described by Weber, to whom Mannheim himself was indebted. "No historian who wants to explain American development or American institutions," Hofstadter has written, "will want to neglect the fundamentally Protestant character of American society. . . . Nor will he, without necessarily embracing all of Max Weber's debatable thesis about the Protestant ethic, fail to consider the possible role of the Protestant dynamic and Protestant economic morale."[16]

The persistence and vitality of the Protestant ethic have been Hofstadter's central interest as an intellectual historian. The Protestant economic morale—individualism, the sanctity of private property, thrift, and industry as virtues identified with the inner-worldly ideology of capitalism—and the Protestant dynamic, an emphasis on moral values associated with other-worldly perfectionism, have been the underpinnings of the ideology he has wished to end. Like Mannheim and the Progressives, Hofstadter has given the intellectual an important role in bringing about this end.

Hofstadter's *Social Darwinism in American Thought* (1944) described the response of late nineteenth-century intellectuals to the economic individualism of Spencerian Darwinism. This doctrine thrived in the Gilded Age because it was congruent with the economic realities of the period: "post-bellum America was like a vast human caricature of the Darwinian struggle for existence and survival of the fittest."[17] Furthermore, Social Darwinism was reinforced by the Protestant ethic preached by the foremost exponent of laissez-faire government, William Graham Sumner, whose sociology "assumed the industrious, temperate, and frugal man of the Protestant ideal."[18] This conservative philosophy, so congenial to the dominant business class, was attacked by the discontented elements in the society, reformers and intellectuals. Their victory over Social Darwinism, however, was to come only with the appropriate changes in "the material basis of the . . . ideology." Until then, the "reform groups, the systematic ideologists, were not fated to have their way. . . . [However,] if no Utopia was in the making, at least there was a shift away from the free competitive order."[19]

Hofstadter here identified the Protestant ethic with the ideology of laissez-faire capitalism, suited perhaps to the material abundance of the late nineteenth century but not to the economic realities of the depression of the 1930's. Intellectuals, because they stood outside the dominant social order and opposed its values, he identified as utopian or perfectionist. Their role, as Hofstadter said of the Progressive reformers, was to "forge durable intellectual weapons"[20]—specifically pragmatism—against the prevailing ideology.

By 1948 and *The American Political Tradition*, however, Hofstadter, like the other liberal historians, was more critical of pragmatism as a weapon of reform. Contemporary liberalism, he said, was "rudderless and demoralized," for Roosevelt's New Deal measures were merely improvisations without sound philosophical guidelines. As a result, liberalism still retained the capitalistic values of the Protestant ethic—

that "ideology of self-help, free enterprise, competition, and beneficent cupidity"[21] which was increasingly irrelevant to the changing economic and political needs of the country. Liberals still clung, for example, to the Founding Fathers' belief that the citizen of a democracy must be a property owner; Hofstadter noted that although this notion might have been appropriate to 1787, "under modern property relations this maxim demands a drastic restriction of the base of political power."[22] He urged that a "more inclusive and systematic conception of what is happening in the world"[23] be formulated so that the achievement of a fuller political democracy would not be hampered by economic inequalities.

*The American Political Tradition* was also more critical of intellectuals, for Hofstadter felt they had failed to counter the capitalist ideology. There was John Calhoun, for example, who had "the faculty of a brilliant but highly abstract and isolated intellectual, to see things that other men never dreamt of and to deny what was under his nose" and whose critique of capitalism was invalid because it rested on Calhoun's own belief in the sanctity of private property. Hofstadter was also critical of the reformers of the Gilded Age, whom he saw as "intellectuals obsessed with the abstract idea of public service," "isolated and sterile" in their failure to take economic realities into account.[24] But he reserved his harshest judgment for those Progressive intellectuals in politics, Theodore Roosevelt and Woodrow Wilson. Since both men were isolated from the facts of economic inequality by their middle-class background, neither was able to transcend the capitalist ideology or bring about significant economic change. Instead, they indulged themselves in the projection of their own abstract moral values into the political arena;[25] like the Wallace Progressives, they succumbed to other-worldly perfectionism. These two sides of Protestantism

were presented, therefore, as conservative obstacles to reform, and the intellectual's isolation, illustrated by his middle-class status, made him susceptible to both forms of ideology.

Hofstadter's next book, *The Age of Reform* (1955), however, indicated that McCarthyism had forced Hofstadter to
reevaluate this ineffectual, conservative intellectual. In his
analysis of the reform tradition from Populism to the New
Deal, Hofstadter again found within liberalism both varieties of ideology. Populism, prompted by the anachronistic
"agrarian myth" of "personal entrepreneurship and individual opportunity,"[26] represented that inner-worldliness associated with capitalism. In Hofstadter's view it was, therefore,
a conservative rather than a radical political movement.

The Progressives too were motivated by these same irrelevant capitalistic values. Yet the emphasis here was on the
other-worldly strand of Protestant thought: Progressives
"set impossible standards [and] they were victimized by a
form of moral absolutism."[27] Progressivism, moreover, was
very much a movement by and for intellectuals. Hence, Progressives shared the common failings of intellectuals who
traditionally

> suffer from a sense of isolation which they usually seek to
> surmount by finding ways of getting into rapport with
> the people, and they readily succumb to a tendency to
> sentimentalize the folk . . . [and] choose to ignore ele-
> ments of illiberalism that frequently seem to be an in-
> dispensable part of popular movements.[28]

The elements of illiberalism that Hofstadter described—na-
tivism, isolationism, anti-Semitism, and conspiratorial thinking—were those which he later found within McCarthyism.[29]
The most typical of Progressive reforms, therefore, was "the
movement for direct popular democracy" or the "ethos of
political participation without self-interest."[30] Hofstadter al-

so commented ruefully that contemporary political trends "suggest that we are in a certain sense moving closer to the plebiscitarian ideals, the mass democracy, that the advocates of direct government had in mind."[31] Although *The Age of Reform* is usually construed as linking McCarthyism with Populism,[32] Hofstadter actually equated "populistic" democracy with Progressivism, and particularly Progressive intellectuals.

According to this analysis, the intellectual, again isolated from political and economic realities by his middle-class status and compelled by his status to identify himself with an illiberal populace, was once more the conveyor of moral values and perfectionism. Perfectionism, however, was no longer a conservative force, but had spawned McCarthyism, which threatened to overturn the status quo. Perfectionism, in short, was no longer an ideology but a utopia, and the Progressive intellectual was no longer the ineffectual reformer that Hofstadter had examined in *The American Political Tradition* but a dangerous radical and a potential breeder of totalitarianism.

These Progressive intellectuals were contrasted with the New Dealers, who dealt not in moral absolutes but with political and practical realities. The New Dealers, therefore, were "trying . . . to repudiate the European world of ideology."[33] During the New Deal, Hofstadter now found, it was the conservatives, isolated from power, rather than the liberals in power, who were guilty of "utopianism" or "an exalted faith in the intangibles of morals and character."[34] Hofstadter's admission that the political left and the political right had exchanged roles and thought systems[35] was his version of that fusion of the liberal and conservative identities achieved by the new conservatism.

His discussion of the popular hostility toward intellectuals during the McCarthy period also revealed his rejection of his own earlier goal of political democracy and his concept of the intellectual's role as the formulator of utopia. By 1952, Hofstadter explained, the New Deal liberals had been in power for twenty years and had "quite unconsciously taken on the psychology of those who have entered into possession":[36] they had become an elite. As such, they were the targets of the anti-intellectualism characteristic of the right-wing "status politics" practiced by those Americans whom Hofstadter variously described as old Yankees or new immigrants but who were, in essence, the political "outs" or those on the social periphery—in short, the vast majority of the American electorate. Status politics, or as he later called it, "cultural politics," was concerned with values and moral absolutes; it was "destructive and 'radical'" and "[stood] psychologically outside the framework of normal democratic politics, which is largely an affair of compromise." He concluded that "one of the most fundamental qualities . . . in the right-wing mentality of our time is its implicit utopianism."[37]

As Hofstadter developed his concept of status politics in his later essays on the "paranoid style," the destructive radicalism of utopian perfectionism was made explicit. He used Barry Goldwater as an example of a politician who had repudiated the "venerable tradition" of politics based on compromise between interest groups, finding it "vastly inferior to a politics that would address itself to realizing the religious and moral values of the public"; as a result, Hofstadter concluded, he came "as close as any presidential candidate has ever come to subverting the whole pattern of our politics of coalition and consensus."[38]

In terms of this analysis, the intellectuals of the political left, once the isolated opponents of the conservative ideology of capitalism, had become those within the power structure and the opponents of a radical utopia. Hofstadter's *Anti-Intellectualism in American Life* (1963), written when intellectuals were once again in the White House, was a justification for their being there and a further clarification of their new role. Hofstadter pointed out that the Founding Fathers, the men of reason who had established a stable government, provided the historical precedent for the intellectual's current political status. In the period of Jacksonian democracy, however, intellect had become equated with elitism, and intellectuals were removed from positions of political prominence. Although they again played a significant role during the Progressive movement, it was not until the New Deal that intellectuals once more regained their seats of power.

The American distrust of the intellect was perhaps inevitable, given the conditions which Hofstadter found dominant in the American past: "the religion of the heart" or Protestant fundamentalism, stressing emotion over reason; the equalitarian "politics of democracy," hostile to the elitism of intellect and education; the "practical culture" reflecting the influence of business values, which distrusted theoretical speculation; and the American notion of "education in a democracy," which emphasized the development of vocational skills rather than the development of the mind. Yet sometimes, he warned, intellectuals themselves were to blame for their loss of prestige. The Puritan clergy, for example, were denied their former respected status because they became "abstract and highly intellectual."[39] The intellectuals in the early labor movements were also prone to a perfectionism which hindered the growth of unions and earned them the dislike of practical labor leaders.[40] The fall from grace of these intellectuals was like that of the intellectuals during the McCarthy period, who, like Hofstadter himself in the late forties, had become too interested in philosophy and too concerned with moral questions.

To counteract this tendency toward perfectionism, Hofstadter sought, as had Morgan, an inner balance for the intellectual between what he called "piety" and "playfulness."

Piety was his term for the intellectual's responsiveness to abstractions and moral values and his passion for rationality, justice, and order; he saw this as the source of "much of [the intellectual's] value to mankind and, equally, much of his ability to do mischief" since it could lead to rigid perfectionism. Piety must be offset by playfulness, his term for the ability to adapt to changing realities, searching not for abstract truth but for "new certainties" to meet new situations.[41]

Like Morgan's intellectual, Hofstadter's intellectual also faced the "Puritan dilemma." Many intellectuals, Hofstadter found, were uneasy in their current role as political insiders: "perhaps the most divisive issue in the intellectual community today arises over the values to be placed upon the old alienation and the new acceptance."[42] Both positions had drawbacks. The alienated intellectual, outside of the power structure, exhibited an "excessive concern with his own purity"; the intellectual within the system, however, ran the risk that "a sudden association with power [would] become . . . intellectually blinding." These alternatives, Hofstadter concluded, "epitomize the intellectual's own version of the tragic predicament that faces any man who is in one way or another caught between his most demanding ideals and his more immediate ambitions and interests."[43]

Hofstadter suggested that this dualism be exchanged for a type of pluralism in which a number of roles would be open to the intellectual. But his own choice is implicit in his adherence to Mannheim's epistemology. For although a position outside the going order was necessary if the intellectual was to act as watchman in the "pitch-black night," political participation was necessary to achieve knowledge of the needs of society. From this point of view, the isolation of intellectuals, as Hofstadter showed in *Social Darwinism* and *The American Political Tradition,* led to futility. From *The Age of Reform* on, moreover, Hofstadter was concerned with showing that isolation led to the dangerous ideological politics of perfectionism.

Therefore he chose his own version of life in the world—the intellectual as political "expert," as exemplified in the New Deal Brain Trust. In this capacity the intellectual would perform a "distinct and necessary function in the national scheme of things" by virtue of "certain serviceable skills."[44] The role of the university, as in the "Wisconsin plan" during the Progressive period, would be to provide "not propaganda or ideologies, but information, statistics, advice, skills and training."[45] Ironically, Hofstadter, who had repeatedly maintained that the life of the mind was valuable for its own sake and who had criticized the excessively practical orientation of the American business culture and American education, now saw the intellect as a tool that could be put to practical use.

The redefinition of the role of the intellectual as a furnisher of utopias which he once shared with the Progressives was completed with Hofstadter's final act of intellectual parricide in *The Progressive Historians* (1968). Beard, Turner, and Parrington, he said, were the men who had initially made history seem worth studying, for they had turned their talents and historical analyses to the cause of reform. Yet they had equated political democracy with equalitarianism and absolute moral values,[46] because they were sadly out of touch with economic and psychological realities; therefore, their reforms went awry, as the mass democracy of McCarthyism had shown.

In this context, Hofstadter finally evaluated the function of the historian or the intellectual. He argued the case for the historian *engagé* or the historian as "embattled participant."[47] He did not mean, however, that the Progressive historians, who were certainly *engagé*, were to provide the models for contemporary intellectuals. Beard, he said, "became our supreme tragic example of the activist mind in history," referring to what he felt was Beard's ill-considered criticism of Roosevelt's attempt to involve the United States in World War II.[48] Engagement here did not mean the active attempt to change the world, to bring about reforms such as the Progressives had envisioned; it meant, on the contrary, a keener sense of the social and moral complexities of human history—an awareness of "defeat and failure" which the Progressives had lacked. Quoting Boorstin, Hofstadter concluded that most of human history has been a "disproving ground for utopias."[49] Since history had disproved the Progressives' utopia, it had also disproved their faith in the utopian intellectual.

Hofstadter began his career by wishing to "end" the ideology of capitalism in order to further political democracy; the intellectual was to furnish the political philosophy and the moral goals to bring this about. The role he later came to choose for the intellectual, however, has made this aim impossible, for the inclusion of the man of reason within the political power structure has redefined his purpose. He is no longer to supply the philosophical alternative to ideology, as he did in the late nineteenth-century setting Hofstadter described in *Social Darwinism in American Thought*. Nor is he to provide those moral absolutes which could too easily become weapons against him, as had the participatory democracy of the Progressives. The intellectual as expert would deal with "grave and intricate problems of power"[50] and with economics, the sole legitimate concern of the democratic process; morality and philosophy have no place in this scheme.

For the Progressives, reason and moral values were the intellectual's tools for reform. With their removal, the possibility of change is likewise eliminated. The intellectual, ensconced within the dominant class, is no longer the reform-

er, but the supporter of the status quo, whose basic compo-
nent is, as Hofstadter has repeatedly pointed out, capitalism.
The intellectual, to escape utopian perfectionism, has become the ideologue of capitalism.

## NOTES

1. "Letter from Washington," *New Yorker* 36 (February 4, 1961): 108, 109.
2. Ibid., p. 108.
3. "Failure and Challenge," *The New Leader* 44 (July 3 and 10, 1961): 5.
4. "The President and Other Intellectuals," *American Scholar* 30 (Autumn, 1961): 516.
5. George Lichtheim, "The Role of the Intellectuals," *Commentary* 29 (April, 1960): 295–307.
6. Richard S. Kirkendall, "Franklin D. Roosevelt and the Service Intellectuals," *Journal of American History* 49 (December, 1962): 471.
7. *Ideology and Utopia: An Introduction to the Sociology of Knowledge,* trans. Louis Wirth and Edward Shils (New York: Harcourt, Brace, and World, n.d.), p. xxi.
8. Ibid., p. 40.
9. Richard Hofstadter, "History and the Social Sciences," in *The Varieties of History, from Voltaire to the Present,* ed. Fritz Stern (New York: Meridian Books, 1959), p. 362.
10. *Ideology and Utopia,* p. 164.
11. Ibid., p. 31. Describing Herbert Hoover's refusal to abandon his belief in laissez-faire government in the face of the exigencies of the Depression, Hofstadter quoted Mannheim: "nothing is more removed from actual events than the closed rational system. Under certain circumstances nothing contains more irrational drive than a fully self-contained, intellectualistic world-view" (*The American Political Tradition and the Men Who Made It* [New York: Vintage Books, 1957], p. 149).
12. *Ideology and Utopia,* p. 31.
13. Ibid., p. 155.
14. Ibid., pp. 159, 161.
15. Ibid., p. 258.
16. *The Progressive Historians: Turner, Beard, and Parrington* (New York: Alfred A. Knopf, 1968), p. 161.

17. *Social Darwinism in American Thought, 1860–1915* (Philadelphia: University of Pennsylvania Press, 1944), p. 30.

18. Ibid., p. 37.

19. Ibid., p. 98.

20. Ibid., p. 145.

21. Hofstadter, *The American Political Tradition*, p. vii.

22. Ibid., p. 16.

23. Ibid., p. 352.

24. Ibid., pp. 91, 177.

25. Hofstadter's idea that the politician projects into the political arena his own personal needs is borrowed from Harold Lasswell. As Hofstadter explained it, "According to Lasswell, [the politician's] private motives are frequently diverted to public objects and rationalized by the individual into public ideologies" (Richard Hofstadter and Beatrice Hofstadter, "Winston Churchill: A Study in the Popular Novel," *American Quarterly* 2 [Spring, 1950]: 15–16). On p. 211 of *The American Political Tradition*, Hofstadter suggested that Theodore Roosevelt had "a persistent desire to impose himself upon others. Such a personal motive, projected into public affairs, easily became transformed into the imperial impulse." On p. 238, Hofstadter said of Wilson: "Capable himself of intense feelings of guilt, he projected his demand for unmitigated righteousness into public affairs." Lasswell's theory is also important to Hofstadter's notion of "status politics."

26. *The Age of Reform from Bryan to F.D.R.* (New York: Alfred A. Knopf, 1955), p. 11.

27. Ibid., p. 16.

28. Ibid., pp. 18–19.

29. Hofstadter, "The Pseudo-Conservative Revolt," in *The Radical Right*, ed. Daniel Bell (Garden City and New York: Anchor Books, 1964), esp. pp. 91–92.

30. *The Age of Reform*, p. 259.

31. Ibid., p. 268.

32. See, for example, Michael Paul Rogin, *McCarthy and the Intellectuals: The Radical Spectre* (Cambridge, Mass., and London: M.I.T. Press, 1967); or Norman Pollack, *The Populist Response to Industrial America* (New York: W. W. Norton Co., 1962).

33. *The Age of Reform*, p. 325.

34. Ibid., p. 315.

35. Ibid.

36. "The Pseudo-Conservative Revolt," p. 75.

37. "Pseudo-Conservatism Revisited," in *The Radical Right*, pp. 101–2.

38. *The Paranoid Style in American Politics and Other Essays* (New York: Alfred A. Knopf, 1965), pp. 121, 103.

39. *Anti-Intellectualism in American Life* (New York: Alfred A. Knopf, 1963), p. 65.

40. Ibid., pp. 282–83.

41. Ibid., pp. 28–29, 30.

42. Ibid., p. 393.

43. Ibid., pp. 429, 417.

44. Ibid., p. 196.

45. Ibid., p. 200.

46. *The Progressive Historians*, pp. 126–27, 248.

47. Ibid., p. 466.

48. Ibid., p. 464.

49. Ibid., pp. 466, 450.

50. *Anti-Intellectualism in American Life*, p. 401.

# CHAPTER 7

# "WE HAD NO DREAM TO LOSE"

The violence and political dissent of the 1960's sharply challenged the liberal historians' claims for the "end of ideology." The search for consensus, stability, and American uniqueness seemed to have ended in disaster; intellectuals had again succumbed to perfectionism. The historical realities of this decade, moreover, revealed the vast gap between the appearance and the reality of liberal history and illustrated the hollowness of the liberal celebration of a nonideological liberalism.

The decade had opened hopefully, for the election of John F. Kennedy after the stifling Eisenhower years represented the promise of youth to aging and disillusioned liberals. When the promise was tragically cut down,[1] liberalism seemed suddenly older. Yet the peaceful accession to power of Vice-President Lyndon Johnson and his evident desire for the consensus which liberals valued was temporarily reassuring.[2] The consensus was briefly threatened by what appeared to be a revival of the ideological right in Barry Goldwater's presidential campaign in 1964,[3] but liberal fears were dispelled by Goldwater's overwhelming defeat at the polls.

No sooner had the challenge on the right been met, however, than the liberal center was assaulted by the political left. The rediscovery of hunger and want in an affluent society, publicized in Michael Harrington's *The Other America* (1962) and officially recognized in Johnson's War on Poverty

in 1964, revived doubts about the beneficence of liberal capitalism. The Negro drive for civil rights became increasingly
militant, even after the Civil Rights Act of 1964, culminating
in a wave of rioting in the urban black ghettos and creating
the fear of a white backlash. A nation still stunned by the assassination of John Kennedy was further horrified by the
murders in 1968 of his brother Robert and of Martin Luther
King, head of the Southern Christian Leadership Confer-
ence. Perhaps most important, opposition to the war in Vietnam increased with Johnson's bombing of North Vietnam in
early 1965. The increasing dissatisfaction of college students,
both with the escalation of the war and with the administration of their universities, was evidenced by the growth of
Students for a Democratic Society, by student disorders
across the country, and by the shutting-down of Columbia,
Harvard, and Cornell universities in 1968 and 1969.[4] In the
spring of 1970, the invasion of American troops into Cambo-
dia precipitated nationwide student protests, culminating
in the death of four students at Kent State University and
the closing of almost all the major universities in the country.
     Out of the political and social atmosphere of the sixties
sprang the New Left, the first significant intellectual challenge to postwar liberalism and the most recent embodiment
of the liberal concept of ideological politics. Spawned by the
aborted hopes of the Kennedy administration, the young
self-styled radicals openly sought an ideology or a utopia,
with participatory democracy—"power to the people"—as
their rallying cry; products of an affluent society, they were
less motivated by economic goals than aroused by the moral
issues of civil rights, peace, and the poverty amid affluence.
Hostile to a political and economic system which perpetuated racism and poverty at home while conducting an im-
moral war in Southeast Asia, the New Left made threaten-
ing gestures at the status quo and aroused divisive conflict

within liberal strongholds like the universities and the Democratic party. Because the new radicalism existed almost entirely within the context of higher education, this seemed further proof to liberals that the intellectual was particularly prone to ideology.

The New Left, further, demanded a reassessment of a liberalism which seemed as inadequate and as culpable in the face of the realities of the 1960's as Progressivism had seemed to the liberals themselves in the 1930's. The young radicals, therefore, launched a frontal assault upon liberal thought in much the same way that the liberals had attacked their own predecessors, and on the same grounds: liberalism's conservatism and its view of human nature. The disillusion with liberalism was best summarized by Thomas Hayden, a past president of the Students for a Democratic Society:

> There is, I find, an inhibiting, dangerous conservative temperament behind the facade of liberal realism which is so current: Niebuhr in theology; Kornhauser, Lipset, and Bell in political science and sociology; the neo-Freudians in psychology; Hofstadter in history; Schlesinger and others of the A.D.A. mind in the Democratic Party. Their themes purport to be different but always the same themes emerge: Man is inherently incapable of building a good society; man's passionate causes are nothing more than dangerous psychic sprees (the issues of this period too complex and sensitive to be colored by emotionalism or moral conviction); ideals have little place in politics.[5]

Much of New Left criticism has been directed at the liberal "end of ideology." Fearful of the mass emotions which ideology had proved capable of unleashing for totalitarian movements, liberals, according to this analysis, had rejected not only ideology but utopia, creating the "dangers of a placid acceptance of the given."[6] More specifically, this rejection "separated ethics from politics" and ruled out of the political sphere "revolutionary values" and "ultimate questions of justice." Politics was reduced to an economic process, concerned solely with the distribution of material goods; hence, liberal complacency glorified an unjust and amoral capitalism.[7]

If liberals had judged the Progressives too unrealistic about man, radicals found the liberal too "realistic." By accepting as a prescriptive norm the empirical findings that showed the democratic citizen less interested in political issues and political participation than he should be, the liberals' elitist version of democracy by and for the well-placed and well-off meant "the practical abandonment of what has been the distinctive moral function of democratic politics and government," the "general attainment of the ideal of rational, active, and informed democratic man."[8] New Leftists insisted that the confusion of what is with what ought to be in the realm of democratic politics was ultimately self-defeating.[9] Radicals asked, therefore, for a "new infusion of utopian idealism" into politics and for the return of ideology, or the application of intelligence to "the human condition and its betterment in an always imperfect world."[10]

The goal of New Left history has been this search for ideology and utopian idealism in the past and for a legitimate historical basis for their own radicalism. Just as the liberals rewrote Progressive history, the New Left has cast aside the liberal version of the past. Staughton Lynd, for example, examining the "intellectual origins of American radicalism," found an "unbroken continuity between the revolutionaries of 1776 and twentieth-century radicals,"[11] a rebuttal to Morgan's interpretation of the Revolution as a conservative movement by and for property owners. Norman Pollack, openly quarreling with Hofstadter's analysis of Populism in

*The Age of Reform*, claimed that Populism, although it shared some perspectives with Marx, was a significant indigenous radical movement.[12] American Socialism was a viable political force which pushed the Progressives to the left, argued Kenneth McNaught,[13] challenging Hartz' contention in *The Liberal Tradition* that the alternatives to the liberal consensus were futile. The rediscovery of important radical ideologies was an attempt to overturn the liberal notion of the American consensus on political values. The New Left has also sought to undermine the liberal image of the American as the bourgeois capitalist by stressing class conflict as a historical force and by placing a new emphasis on the role of minority groups in American history, particularly blacks and women.[14]

Coupled with this rewriting of liberal historiography has been the New Left's attack on the liberal version of the role of the intellectual. The most common charge has been that the liberal intellectual has sold out to the "establishment"— the federal government or the prestigious universities—and has, therefore, relinquished his proper role as social critic.[15] Repudiating the elitism which "glorifies intellectuals . . . as experts and social technicians," Christopher Lasch accused liberal historians of becoming "apologists . . . for American national power in the holy war against communism" and the "servants of bureaucratic power." "In the last twenty years," Lasch maintained, "the elitism of intellectuals has expressed itself as a celebration of American life."[16] The intellectual, according to the New Left, must remain outside the power structure to retain his critical independence. He must also, however, involve himself in the political and moral issues of the time, and his written history must reflect contemporary problems. Although this role bears a surface resemblance to Hofstadter's concept of the historian as "embattled participant," involvement for the young radicals does not mean

writing history which illustrates the futility of utopian perfectionism, as it does for the liberals, but finding in the past
an alternative and better vision of the future.[17]

These young historians have thus far been more successful
as critics than as reshapers of liberal historiography. For the
thrust of New Left history reveals that it is captive to the
liberal tradition, which still provides the questions to be
asked and answered. There appear to be two reasons for this.
First, New Left history is a relatively recent phenomenon,
with few major publications before the mid-sixties. It took
the liberal historians almost twenty years to make their final
break with the Progressives, even though this split was has-
tened by the McCarthy period. There is no reason to sup-
pose that the New Left will establish its own intellectual
identity in much less time, although here the Vietnam War
provides the added impetus. Second and more important, although always brusque and sometimes intentionally rude,
the young radicals have in fact been too respectful of their
elders. For they have taken the liberal historians at their
word, and a literal reading of their work has trapped the
New Left into giving too much credence to its surface meaning and interpreting the liberals as complacent celebrants of
a placid past and present.

The difficulties of a literal interpretation of their history
are illustrated by the liberal historians' own response to the
1960's. Their message is the same: nonideological liberalism
is responsible for the American consensus, the stability of
American institutions, and American uniqueness. But there
has been a perceptible shift in emphasis in keeping with the
changing political temper of the decade. For example, Hofstadter's *American Violence* (1970), reflecting the contemporary concern with ghetto riots, assassinations, and student
strikes, maintained that although violence is a commonplace
in our past, it has not traditionally embodied a revolutionary

challenge to the legitimacy of the federal government; hence, our political institutions have been able to maintain "a long record of basic political stability."[18] In fact, Hofstadter found that violence—from the suppression of slave insurrections to the 1968 Chicago police action against student protesters at the Democratic convention—has been the weapon of those who wished to retain the status quo or uphold majority value systems. What was frightening about the 1960's, however, was that violence was being preached and practiced by a political left which had cast aside as irrelevant the traditional liberal method of gradual and peaceful reform. Given the traditional American use of coercion by the political right, Hofstadter feared that violence by the left would lead to the use of counterforce and to the political repression of dissent.[19]

Theoretically, of course, there is no place for violent political disagreement within a historical framework which finds consensus on the fundamental values of liberalism, and Hofstadter's tacit suggestion that the status quo has been maintained by coercion is startling from a historian who has maintained that American political conflicts have been sham battles. Yet violence is implicit in Hofstadter's history, as it is in the history of his contemporaries. As he himself noted, his thinking was initially shaped by the violent clash of ideologies at home and abroad in the 1930's, the domestic turbulence of the Depression decade and the terrorism of European fascism. World War II and the Korean War, conceived of as wars against totalitarian ideologies, were of course violent. The ideological politics of McCarthyism, while it did not culminate in the use of physical force, created violent controversy and retaliation upon the left by the conservative majority of just the sort that Hofstadter feared in 1970.

Schlesinger was also concerned with violence in the late sixties and found that its current manifestations were attributable to the fact of more or less constant warfare for over a generation and to the celebration of violence by the mass media, particularly television.[20] But as for Hofstadter, violence is no new discovery for Schlesinger, for it plays a central role in the view of human nature he has borrowed from Niebuhr: man has an inbred instinct for violence which cannot be quelled, and it would be utopian not to realize this.[21] However, Schlesinger concluded, violence "is justified only when the resources of reason are demonstrably exhausted and when the application of force remains the only way of achieving rational ends."[22] But since Schlesinger has also repeatedly told us that man is inherently irrational, violence is inevitable. This is why Schlesinger's vision of the liberal consensus is less the vital center than the terrified middle ground between the violence-breeding ideologies of the left and the right. Schlesinger's interpretation of the New Deal, central to everything he has written, was that it rescued the American political and economic system from the dual apocalypse threatened by radical Communism and the reactionary Liberty League; *The Age of Roosevelt* is suffused with Schlesinger's dire suspicion that the country was saved from revolution only by Roosevelt's liberal middle way. Under the outwardly placid surface of nonideological consensus history, then, lie the terrors of ideological politics, the constant fear of political conflict and violence created by the unruly and irrational American mob.

If the difficulties of the consensus interpretation of liberal historiography are poignantly revealed by the realities of the 1960's, so are the contradictions in liberal assertions about the stability of American institutions. For example, Boorstin's own response to the 1960's was a collection of essays entitled *The Decline of Radicalism* (1969). The title in itself sounds peculiar from a historian who has never admitted that radicalism existed in this country. His reference, however, was to the militant black and student-power groups, which he saw as the threat to the community upon which American social and political stability rested.[23] How this admittedly tiny fraction of Americans could endanger the stability of a nation which had earlier survived a full-scale Revolution and a bloody Civil War is a mystery. Perhaps these radicals are dangerous because, as Boorstin suggested, twentieth-century communities are "more numerous and more pervasive" but also "thinner, more volatile, more transient" than those of earlier periods. This suggestion follows logically from Boorstin's reliance upon his "consumption community," held together not by man's reason or moral values but by the self-interest of Horatio Alger, who contains within himself the seeds of chaos and disorder. Ironically, Boorstin concluded that "some of our fellow Americans go in desperate search of communities, though communities can never be the product of desperation."[24] But his own community was the product of desperation, bred of the fear of destructive ideology or utopia which would rend the fabric of civil society; this community cannot provide stability for a social and political order which perpetually hovers, as Boorstin's does, on the brink of disaster because it is threatened by irrational and selfish man. Boorstin has attempted to strengthen his community by filling it with institutions instead of people, but since institutions, by definition, are unchanging entities, his history describes not stability, but stasis. This analysis is clearly a-historical.

The analysis of historical change by the other liberal historians also belies the stability of the American past which they purportedly describe; in reality, there is no smooth transition between one historical period and the next, but a series of vast and disruptive crises which in turn precipitate other crises. Schlesinger's *Crisis of Confidence* (1969) was preceded by his *Crisis of the Old Order* and *The Politics of*

*Upheaval.* Morgan explained the coming of the American Revolution in *The Stamp Act Crisis.* Or here is Hofstadter, explaining the sudden growth of late nineteenth-century imperialism in what he considered a traditionally isolationist America: there was, he said, "a relationship between an observable crisis in the national consciousness and the events of the [Spanish-American] war. . . . America's entrance into the Philippine Islands was a by-product of the . . . war. The Philippine crisis is inseparable from a larger constellation that might be called 'the psychic crisis' of the 1890's."[25] This reliance upon the crisis theory of historical change is necessitated by liberals' assertions about the stability and continuity of the American past, but what this analysis actually tells us is that change in the status quo leads to change in the status quo. In terms of causal explanation, this is not very illuminating. Moreover, this approach denies not only that stable past associated with liberal historiography, but even the minimal continuity necessary to explain the causal relationship of one historical event to another.

If the liberals must have grave doubts about their claims for the American consensus or American stability, they must have as little confidence in the uniqueness of American liberalism which they have also preached. The belief that the American past and present are in some way distinctive and immune to the problems of Europe is as old as Puritan historiography and was most forcefully expressed by Frederick Jackson Turner. Yet although these historians criticize Turner on the grounds that he underestimated European influences in the New World,[26] their common fear that this country would become caught up in the ideological politics of Europe has led them to describe as unique certain American institutions or characteristics. Hartz, Boorstin, and Morgan simply restate in more sophisticated terms Turner's idea about free land and material abundance as being peculiarly American. For Hofstadter, uniqueness lies in the American two-party system;[27] for Schlesinger, perhaps in the distinctively American pragmatic temperament. Yet while all proclaim that this country is different, they operate with theories designed to explain European situations: Niebuhr and Fromm on European totalitarianism, or Weber and Mannheim on the relationship between religious and political idea systems and the European social setting. Even Tocqueville's analysis of Jacksonian democracy was written with the French Revolution of 1789 in mind. While the virtue of comparative analysis lies in added perspective, the dangers of applying theories out of social, political, and economic context are obvious. More obvious is the folly of proclaiming American uniqueness while working with European models.

Because its counter-Progressive thrust has been obvious, it is often assumed, especially by the liberal historians themselves, that their work represents a methodological improvement over that of the Progressives. In fact, however, the rejection of the Progressive belief in man's rationality makes greater methodological sophistication impossible. For example, the liberals are primarily intellectual historians who claim that they, unlike the Progressives, take ideas seriously.[28] Yet the problems of writing intellectual history about irrational man are insuperable. Boorstin and Morgan, believing that man's reason can perceive only his self-interest, ultimately write not the history of man's ideas but of his pocketbook. Hofstadter, on the other hand, operates on the premise that his subjects' words indicate unconscious drives; he has, therefore, read into these words what he has thought they meant and has used "political rhetoric to get at political pathology."[29] He then describes not political theory but the "paranoid style" of American politics, much in the way that Hartz describes liberal thought as a neurotic reflex to

psychological isolation. For Hartz to complain that there is
no American political philosophy is the crowning irony, for
philosophy cannot be created by men who react instead of
think.

Liberals are also fond of accusing Progressives of over-
simplifying historical causation by relying upon economic
analysis. Hence, Morgan writes of the American Revolution
that "a little close inspection reveals such a tangle of forces
at work that even the most obvious change cannot be explained"; and Boorstin notes that the historian "who has
handled the remains . . . knows how imperfectly he has understood their living complexity."[30] Hofstadter too has spoken
of the "rediscovery of the complexity of American history"
and has criticized Beard for artificially separating economic
interest and ideas, which are in reality inseparable.[31] Yet the
liberal historians themselves have described a liberalism
resting upon an equally oversimplified duality: ideas and interests, idealism and realism, reason and nature, other-
worldly and inner-worldly, utopia and ideology. Further,
when the scale is heavily weighted on the side of the "reality" of man's self-interest, his self-seeking nature, and the
virtues of inner-worldly capitalism, the liberal equilibrium
between these artificial dichotomies will inevitably collapse,
degenerating into a single-factor economic interpretation of
the past. More important, the removal of idealism, reason,
and other-worldly utopias results in the ethical relativism so
apparent in liberal thought.

Apologists for liberal history frequently discuss its "revul-
sion against [the] determinism"[32] presumably implicit in the
Progressive emphasis on economics. This comment is accu-
rate only insofar as these liberals explain change in terms of
disconnected and arbitrarily caused crises. For in fact their
view of man is inherently deterministic. Take, for example,
Schlesinger's *Crisis of Confidence*, which, he said, refers to

the loss of "placid faith in our virtue and our invulnerabil-
ity. . . . Events seem to have slipped beyond our control; we
have lost our immunity to history."[33] We wonder when
Schlesinger's liberal—Brownson, Franklin Roosevelt, or Kennedy—ever had any control over events, when he was not
subject to the vicissitudes of history. In an intellectual context in which man is irrational, he has no control over his
fate. Thus, his thought and actions are determined by his
social setting—being "born free" or being in or out of the
"world," the "community," or the power structure. Schlesinger's liberal, like Hartz' Horatio Alger, is at the mercy of
his environment. Boorstin's businessman does not change nature but adapts to its exigencies; Hofstadter's intellectual,
enmeshed in the establishment, can at best provide a justification for it. Morgan finally admits to a form of economic
determinism that he had shunned in the Progressives.[34] The
liberals, because they rejected the perfectionist idealism of
the Progressive history, have succumbed to the determinism
and materialism which it escaped.

Finally, the attempt to wed liberalism to capitalism has
not convinced the American populace, their fellow intellectuals, or the liberal historians themselves of the terrors of
ideological or utopian politics. This is again made apparent
in their discussion of the realities of the 1960's. Boorstin,
writing in the anguished aftermath of the killing of the four
Kent State University students, complained that Americans
were becoming "hypochondriacs," worrying about imaginary
ills within our society because they were comparing it with
some imaginary utopia. He implied that the Americans of the
1970's, unlike those of earlier ages, were becoming utopians.[35]
Yet the whole thrust of his history has been to disprove ideologies and utopias—Blackstone's, Jefferson's, Henry Wallace's, or Joseph McCarthy's. Like that of his colleagues,
Boorstin's work has been an outcry against the utopianism

of American thought which he simultaneously claimed did not exist.

Schlesinger too worried about the "new hostility to politics" on the part of New Left intellectuals, and he furnished examples to prove that the marriage of intellectuals with power has been a fruitful and long-lasting one in our past.[36] But surely it is not just the radical intellectuals of today who fear that power will corrupt them and are given to imposing their own moral standards upon politics.[37] According to Schlesinger himself, there is nothing "new" about this. All his history, like Morgan's and Hofstadter's, is directed explicitly at erring utopian intellectuals who have rejected power for the sake of intellectual purity—Orestes Brownson, the Transcendentalists, the Progressives of both the early and the late varieties. Schlesinger is simply finding in the 1960's still other examples of the perfectionist intellectuals about whom he has written so much.

The realities of the last decade also allow us to reevaluate these historians' assessment of their own role. The liberals have prided themselves on being the pragmatic judges of men and values, on eschewing the moral absolutes of ideology and utopia. Yet their own work is highly charged with the moral purpose of finding a workable liberal tradition and role for the liberal/intellectual, and places before man the agonizing Puritan dilemma of clinging to his ideals in a world which constantly defeats them. Liberal historiography, then, is a moralistic injunction, a value-laden jeremiad designed to provide norms of thought and conduct.

These standards insist upon a liberalism congruent with historical reality and with a realistic assessment of man. And fearing man's belief in his perfectibility, these historians have enjoined liberals to accept the realities of life as it is. The message is conservative but hardly realistic, for it pretends to ignore the perpetual threat of ideological politics which serves as its initial stimulus. Although the events of the sixties prove this perhaps most conclusively because they are most recent, any decade would have done the same.

There never was any liberal consensus, for it was repeatedly challenged by both the left and the right from the 1930's to the 1970's. Nor was there social, economic, or political stability during the Depression, World War II, or the Cold War. There can be nothing unique about American liberalism when its definition was shaped by events abroad. Liberal historiography does not improve upon that of the Progressives by discarding what was good and valuable in it and repeating its mistakes. Liberals and intellectuals, like other people, will continue to be utopians. Although the liberal historians deny all this, this is what in reality they have said.

They have committed the intellectual sin of writing a history which they cannot have believed in, but they have done it in a good cause. "We had no dream to lose,"[38] said Schlesinger of his "realistic" generation. But even this was not true, for they did have a dream of a greater political democracy resting upon a fairer distribution of wealth. This dream was not destroyed by totalitarianism, or by Henry Wallace, or even by Joseph McCarthy, for it was never possible of attainment. Democracy cannot operate without a faith in man's reason, nor will wealth be shared equally if man is inherently self-interested; there can be no balance of realism and idealism if man is not a moral creature. So despite its surface meaning, liberal history has shown us that the vitality of the liberal tradition lies not in its unreasoning and amoral alliance with capitalism, but in its belief in man's capabilities and a better world.

## NOTES

1. James Reston, "What Was Killed Was Not Only the President but the Promise," in *American Politics Since 1945*, ed. Richard Dalfiume (Chicago: Quadrangle Books, 1969), pp. 139–50.

2. Eric F. Goldman, *The Tragedy of Lyndon Johnson* (New York: Alfred A. Knopf, 1969), pp. 51–56 and passim.

3. For the liberal reaction to Goldwater, see Richard Hofstadter, "Goldwater and His Party: The True Believer and the Radical Right," *Encounter* 23 (October, 1964): 3–13; "The Goldwater Débâcle," *Encounter* 24 (January, 1965): 66–70; or "Some Comments on Senator Goldwater," *Partisan Review* 31 (Fall, 1964): 590–92.

4. A good discussion of violence in the 1960's is Jerome H. Skolnick, *The Politics of Protest* (New York: Ballantine Books, 1969).

5. "A Letter to the New (Young) Left," in *The New Student Left: An Anthology*, ed. Mitchell Cohen and Dennis Hale (Boston: Beacon Press, 1966), p. 4.

6. Dennis Wrong, "Reflections on the End of Ideology," *Dissent* 7 (Summer, 1960): 287, 291.

7. Stephen Rousseas and James Farganis, "The Retreat of the Idealists," *The Nation* 196 (March 23, 1963): 240; Michael Paul Rogin, *The Intellectuals and McCarthy: The Radical Spectre* (Cambridge, Mass., and London: M.I.T. Press, 1967), p. 13.

8. Lane Davis, "The Cost of Realism: Contemporary Restatements of Democracy," *Western Political Quarterly* 17 (March, 1964): 37, 39. A good analysis of the liberal restatement of democratic theory is Peter Bachrach, *The Theory of Democratic Elites: A Critique* (Boston: Little, Brown and Co., 1967).

9. Peter Bachrach, *The Theory of Democratic Elites*, pp. 99–100.

10. Carey McWilliams, Foreword to *The New Student Left*, p. x; Rousseas and Farganis, "The Retreat of the Idealists," p. 241.

11. *Intellectual Origins of American Radicalism* (New York: Pantheon Books, 1968), p. 8.

12. *The Populist Response to Industrial America* (New York: W. W. Norton Co., 1962).

13. "American Progressives and the Great Society," *Journal of American History* 53 (December, 1966): 504–20.

14. See, for example, Jesse Lemisch, "Jack Tar in the Streets: Merchant Seamen in the Politics of Revolutionary America," *William and Mary Quarterly* 3rd ser. (July, 1968): 371–407; Staughton Lynd, *Class Conflict, Slavery and the United States Constitution* (Indianapolis: The Bobbs-Merrill Co., 1967); or *Towards a New Past: Dissenting Essays in American History,* ed. Barton Bernstein (New York: Pantheon Books, 1968).

15. Charles Forcey, *The Crossroads of Liberalism: Croly, Weyl, Lippman and the Progressive Era, 1900–1925* (New York: Oxford University Press, 1961), esp. pp. 310–11; Frank A. Warren III, *Liberals and Communism: The "Red Decade" Revisited* (Bloomington and London: Indiana University Press, 1966), p. 233 and passim.

16. "The Cultural Cold War: A Short History of the Congress for Cultural Freedom," in *Towards a New Past,* pp. 338, 323, 344, 358.

17. Staughton Lynd, "Historical Past and Existential Present," in *The Dimensions of History,* ed. Thomas N. Guinsberg (Chicago: Rand McNally and Co., 1970), pp. 73–80; or Howard Zinn, *The Politics of History* (Boston: Beacon Press, 1970).

18. Richard Hofstadter and Michael Wallace, eds., *American Violence: A Documentary History* (New York: Alfred A. Knopf, 1970), p. 10.

19. Ibid., pp. 29–43.

20. Arthur M. Schlesinger, Jr., *The Crisis of Confidence: Ideas, Power, and Violence in America* (Boston: Houghton Mifflin, 1969), pp. 25–32.

21. Ibid., p. 50.

22. Ibid., p. 32.

23.  Daniel J. Boorstin, *The Decline of Radicalism: Reflections on America Today* (New York: Random House, 1969), pp. 121–34.

24.  Ibid., pp. xiv, xv.

25.  *The Paranoid Style in American Politics, and Other Essays* (New York: Alfred A. Knopf, 1965), pp. 146–48.

26.  Hofstadter, *The Progressive Historians: Turner, Beard, and Parrington* (New York: Alfred A. Knopf, 1968), pp. 129–30.

27.  "Political Parties," in *The Comparative Approach to American History*, ed. C. Vann Woodward (New York and London: Basic Books, 1968), pp. 206–19.

28.  Boorstin, *The Genius of American Politics* (Chicago: University of Chicago Press, 1953), p. 77; Edmund S. Morgan, "The Historians of Early New England," in *The Reinterpretation of Early American History*, ed. Ray Allen Billington (San Marino, Calif.: Huntington Library, 1966), p. 47.

29.  *The Paranoid Style*, p. 6.

30.  Edmund S. Morgan, ed., *The American Revolution: Two Centuries of Interpretation* (Englewood Cliffs, N.J.: Prentice-Hall, 1965), p. 2; Boorstin, Introduction to *The Birth of the Republic, 1763–1789* by Edmund S. Morgan (Chicago: University of Chicago Press, 1956), p. vii.

31.  *The Progressive Historians*, pp. 442, 244–45.

32.  John Higham et al., *History* (Englewood Cliffs, N.J.: Prentice-Hall, 1965), p. 220; Jack P. Greene, *The Reappraisal of the American Revolution in Recent Historical Literature* (Baltimore: American Historical Association, 1967); or "The Flight from Determinism: A Review of Recent Literature on the Coming of the American Revolution," *South Atlantic Quarterly* 61 (1962): 235–59.

33.  *The Crisis of Confidence*, p. ix.

34.  Robert Allen Skotheim, *American Intellectual Histories and Historians* (Princeton: Princeton University Press, 1966), p. 276, notes that whereas the Progressive histo-

rians found ideas which hindered change to be environmentally determined, Boorstin and his contemporaries find environment the explanation for ideas which foster stability.

35. "The Spirit of '70," *Newsweek*, July 4, 1970, p. 27.
36. *The Crisis of Confidence*, pp. 89–98.
37. Ibid., p. 89.
38. *The Vital Center: The Politics of Freedom* (Boston: Houghton Mifflin Co., 1949), p. 147.

# BIBLIOGRAPHY

## PRIMARY SOURCES

Boorstin, Daniel J. *America and the Image of Europe: Reflections on American Thought.* Cleveland and New York: World Publishing Co., 1964.

———. *The Americans: The Colonial Experience.* New York: Random House, 1958.

———. *The Americans: The National Experience.* New York: Random House, 1965.

———. *The Decline of Radicalism: Reflections on America Today.* New York: Random House, 1969.

———. "A Dialogue of Two Histories," *Commentary,* 8 (October, 1949), 311–15.

———. "Eggheads Are Their Own Worst Enemies," *New York Times Magazine,* April 26, 1959, p. 5.

———. "The Elusiveness of Mr. Justice Holmes," *New England Quarterly,* 14 (September, 1941), 478–87.

———. "Facade of Our Founding Financiers," *Saturday Review of Literature,* 42 (November 21, 1955), 42–43.

———. *The Genius of American Politics.* Chicago: University of Chicago Press, 1953.

———. *The Image, or What Happened to the American Dream.* New York: Atheneum Publishers, 1962.

———. *The Lost World of Thomas Jefferson.* Boston: Beacon Press, 1960.

———. *The Mysterious Science of the Law.* Cambridge, Mass.: Harvard University Press, 1941.

———. "The New Barbarians," *Esquire*, 70 (October, 1968), 159–62, 260–62.

———. "New View of American Reform," *Commentary*, 21 (April, 1956), 396–98.

———. *The Decline of Radicalism: Reflections on America Today*. New York: Random House, 1969.

———. "The Puritan Tradition: Community Above Ideology," *Commentary*, 26 (October, 1958), 288–99.

———. "Our Unspoken National Faith: Why Americans Need No Ideology," *Commentary*, 15 (April, 1953), 327–37.

———. Review of *The Papers of Thomas Jefferson*, Vol. I, ed. Julian P. Boyd, *William and Mary Quarterly*, 3rd ser. 7 (October, 1950), 596–609.

———. Review of *The Papers of Thomas Jefferson*, Vol. II, ed. Julian P. Boyd, *William and Mary Quarterly*, 3rd ser. 8 (April, 1951), 283–85.

———. Review of *The Papers of Thomas Jefferson*, Vols. IV–VI, ed. Julian P. Boyd, *William and Mary Quarterly*, 3rd ser. 13 (October, 1956), 568–73.

———. "The Spirit of '70," *Newsweek*, July 4, 1970, pp. 27-29.

———. "We, the People, in Quest of Ourselves," *New York Times Magazine*, April 26, 1959, pp. 30, 32, 34.

———. "Welcome to the Consumption Community," *Fortune*, 76 (September 1, 1967), 118–20, 131–38.

———, ed. *An American Primer*. Vol. I. Chicago and London: University of Chicago Press, 1966.

Hartz, Louis. "American Historiography and Comparative Analysis: Further Reflections," *Comparative Studies in Society and History*, 5 (July, 1963), 365–77.

———. "American Political Thought and the American Revolution," *American Political Science Review*, 46 (June, 1952), 321–42.

———. "The Coming of Age in America," *American Political Science Review*, 51 (June, 1957), 474–83.

———. "Comment," *Comparative Studies in Society and History*, 5 (April, 1963), 279–84.

———. "Democracy: Image and Reality." In *Power and Civilization: Political Thought in the Twentieth Century*, ed. David Cooperman and E. V. Walter. New York: Thomas Y. Crowell, 1962.

———. *Economic Policy and Democratic Thought: Pennsylvania, 1776–1860*. Cambridge, Mass.: Harvard University Press, 1948.

———. *The Founding of New Societies*. New York: Harcourt, Brace and World, 1964.

———. *The Liberal Tradition in America: An Interpretation of American Political Thought Since the Revolution*. New York: Harcourt, Brace and Co., 1955.

———. "The Rise of the Democratic Idea." In *Paths of American Thought*, ed. Arthur M. Schlesinger, Jr., and Morton White. Boston: Houghton Mifflin Co., 1963.

———. "South Carolina Versus the United States." In *America in Crisis*, ed. Daniel Aaron. New York: Alfred A. Knopf, 1952.

———. "The Whig Tradition in America and Europe," *American Political Science Review*, 46 (December, 1952), 989–1002.

Hofstadter, Richard. *The Age of Reform from Bryan to F.D.R.* New York: Alfred A. Knopf, 1955.

———. *The American Political Tradition and the Men Who Made It*. New York: Vintage Books, 1957.

———. *Anti-Intellectualism in American Life*. New York: Alfred A. Knopf, 1963.

———. "Beard and the Constitution," *The American Quarterly*, 2 (Fall, 1950), 195–213.

———. "From Calhoun to the Dixiecrats," *Social Research*, 16 (June, 1949), 135–50.

———. "Goldwater and His Party: The True Believer and the Radical Right," *Encounter*, 23 (October, 1964), 3–13.

———. "The Goldwater Débâcle," *Encounter*, 24 (January, 1965), 66–70.

———. "A Historian's View of the Mass Media," *Senior Scholastic*, 70 (February 1, 1957), 5 T.

———. "History and the Social Sciences." In *The Varieties of History from Voltaire to the Present*, ed. Fritz Stern. New York: Meridian Books, 1959.

———. Interview, September 26, 1968. Columbia University.

———. "The Last Refuge," *New Republic*, 114 (May 27, 1946), 779–80.

———. "A Note on Intellect and Power," *American Scholar*, 30 (Autumn, 1961), 588–98.

———. *The Paranoid Style in American Politics and Other Essays*. New York: Alfred A. Knopf, 1965.

———. "Parrington and the Jeffersonian Tradition," *Journal of the History of Ideas*, 11 (October, 1941), 391–400.

———. "Political Parties." In *The Comparative Approach to American History*, ed. C. Vann Woodward. New York and London: Basic Books, 1968. Pp. 206–19.

———. *The Progressive Historians: Turner, Beard, and Parrington*. New York: Alfred A. Knopf, 1968.

———. "Pseudo-Conservatism Revisited." In *The Radical Right*, ed. Daniel Bell. Garden City, N.Y., and New York: Anchor Books, 1964.

———. "The Pseudo-Conservative Revolt." In *The Radical Right*, ed. Daniel Bell. Garden City, N.Y., and New York: Anchor Books, 1964.

———. "Reading the Constitution Anew," *Commentary*, 22 (September, 1956), 270–74.

———. "The Revolution in Higher Education." In *Paths of American Thought*, ed. Arthur M. Schlesinger, Jr., and Morton White. Boston: Houghton Mifflin Co., 1963.

———. "The Right Man for the Big Job," *New York Times Magazine*, April 3, 1960, pp. 121–22.

———. "The Salzburg Seminar, Fourth Year," *Nation*, 171 (October 28, 1950), 391–92.

———. *Social Darwinism in American Thought, 1860–1915*. Philadelphia: University of Pennsylvania Press, 1944.

———. *Social Darwinism in American Thought, 1860–1915*. 2d ed. Boston: Beacon Press, 1955.

———. "Some Comments on Senator Goldwater," *Partisan Review*, 31 (Fall, 1946), 590–92.

———. "Turner and the Frontier Myth," *American Scholar*, 18 (October, 1949), 433–43.

———. "Two Cultures: Adversary and/or Responsible," *The Public Interest*, 6 (Winter, 1967), 68–74.

———. "The 214th Columbia University Commencement Address," *American Scholar*, 37 (Autumn, 1968), 583–89.

———. "U. B. Phillips and the Plantation Legend," *The Journal of Negro History*, 29 (April, 1944), 109–24.

———. "William Leggett, Spokesman of Jacksonian Democracy," *Political Science Quarterly*, 58 (December, 1943), 581–94.

———, ed. *The Progressive Movement, 1900–1915*. Englewood Cliffs, N.J.: Prentice-Hall, 1963.

Hofstadter, Richard, and Handie, D. DeWitt. *The Development and Scope of Higher Education in the United States*. New York: Columbia University Press, 1952.

Hofstadter, Richard, and Hofstadter, Beatrice. "Winston Churchill: A Study in the Popular Novel," *American Quarterly*, 2 (Spring, 1950), 12–18.

Hofstadter, Richard, and Metzger, Walter P. *The Development of Academic Freedom in the United States*. New York: Columbia University Press, 1955.

Hofstadter, Richard, and Wallace, Michael, eds. *American*

*Violence: A Documentary History.* New York: Alfred A. Knopf, 1970.

Morgan, Edmund S. "The American Revolution Considered as an Intellectual Movement." In *Causes and Consequences of the American Revolution,* ed. Esmond Wright. Chicago: Quadrangle Books, 1966.

————. *The American Revolution: A Review of Changing Interpretations.* New York: Macmillan Co., 1958.

————. *The Birth of the Republic, 1763–1789.* Chicago and London: University of Chicago Press, 1956.

————. "Colonial Ideas of Parliamentary Power," *William and Mary Quarterly,* 3rd ser. 5 (July, 1948), 311–41.

————. *The Gentle Puritan: A Life of Ezra Stiles, 1727–1795.* New Haven and London: Yale University Press, 1962.

————. "The Historians of Early New England." In *The Reinterpretation of Early American History,* ed. Ray Allen Billington. San Marino, Calif.: Huntington Library, 1966.

————. "The Labor Problem at Jamestown," *American Historical Review,* 76 (June, 1971), 595–611.

————. "Miller's Williams," *New England Quarterly,* 38 (December, 1965), 513–23.

————. "New England Puritanism: Another Approach," *William and Mary Quarterly,* 3rd ser. 18 (April, 1961), 236–42.

————. *The Puritan Dilemma: The Story of John Winthrop.* Boston and Toronto: Little, Brown and Co., 1958.

————. "The Puritan Ethic and the American Revolution," *William and Mary Quarterly,* 3rd ser. 24 (January, 1967), 3–43.

————. "The Puritan Family and the Social Order," *More Books,* Sixth Series, 38 (January, 1943), 9–21.

————. *The Puritan Family: Religion and Domestic Relations in Seventeenth Century New England.* New York: Harper Torchbooks, 1966.

———. "Puritan Tribalism," *More Books*, 3rd ser. 38 (May, 1943), 203–19.

———. "The Puritans and Sex," *New England Quarterly*, 15 (December, 1942), 591–607.

———. Review of *John Adams and the Prophets of Progress*, by Zoltan Haraszti, *New England Quarterly*, 25 (June, 1952), 274–77.

———. Review of *Religion and Economic Action*, by Kurt Samuelsson, *William and Mary Quarterly*, 3rd ser. 20 (January, 1963), 135–40.

———. Review of *The Winthrop Family in America*, by Lawrence Shaw, *New England Quarterly*, 22 (December, 1949), 532–34.

———. *Roger Williams: The Church and the State.* New York: Harcourt, Brace and World, 1967.

———. "Thomas Hutchinson and the Stamp Act," *New England Quarterly*, 21 (December, 1948), 459–92.

———. *Virginians at Home: Family Life in the Eighteenth Century.* Williamsburg, Va.: Colonial Williamsburg, Inc., 1952.

———. *Visible Saints: The History of a Puritan Idea.* Ithaca, N.Y.: Cornell University Press, 1963.

———. "What Every Yale Freshman Should Know," *Saturday Review*, 43 (January 23, 1960), 13–14.

Morgan, Edmund S., and Morgan, Helen M. *The Stamp Act Crisis: Prologue to Revolution.* Chapel Hill: University of North Carolina Press, 1953.

Schlesinger, Arthur M., Jr. "Adding Guns to E.C.A. Butter," *New Republic*, 119 (November 22, 1948), 19–21.

———. "The Administration and the Left," *New Statesman*, 65 (February 8, 1963), 185–86.

———. *The Age of Jackson.* Boston: Little, Brown and Co., 1950.

———. *The Age of Roosevelt.* Vol. I. *The Crisis of the Old Order, 1919–1933.* Boston: Houghton Mifflin Co., 1957.

——. *The Age of Roosevelt.* Vol. II. *The Coming of the New Deal.* Boston: Houghton Mifflin Co., 1959.

——. *The Age of Roosevelt.* Vol. III. *The Politics of Upheaval.* Boston: Houghton Mifflin Co., 1960.

——. "The Big Game Hunter Who Tamed an Elephant," *Reporter*, 10 (May 25, 1954), 36–38.

——. *The Bitter Heritage: Vietnam and American Democracy, 1941–1966.* Boston: Houghton Mifflin Co., 1967.

——. "The Causes of the Civil War: A Note on Historical Sentimentalism," *Partisan Review*, 16 (1949), 969–81.

——. "Chester Wilmot's War," *The New Statesman and Nation*, 43 (May 10, 1952), 557–59.

——. "The Cold War and the West," *Partisan Review*, 29 (Winter, 1962), 77–81.

——. "Communication," *American Historical Review*, 54 (April, 1949), 785–86.

——. *The Crisis of Confidence: Ideas, Power, and Violence in America.* Boston: Houghton Mifflin Co., 1969.

——. "The Dark Heart of American History," *Saturday Review*, 51 (October 19, 1968), 20–23, 81.

——. "Death Wish of the Democrats," *New Republic*, 139 (September 15, 1958), 7–8.

——. "Democracy, What Does It Mean?" *Vital Speeches of the Day*, 14 (April 15, 1948), 401–2.

——. "Eisenhower Won't Succeed," *New Republic*, 130 (April 5, 1954), 8–12.

——. "Espionage or Frame-Up?" *Saturday Review*, 33 (April 15, 1950), 21–23.

——. "Faith, Fear, and Freedom," *Saturday Review*, 34 (February 3, 1951), 10–11.

——. "Freedom's Enemies," *Saturday Review*, 37 (March 20, 1954), 16–17.

——. "The Future of Liberalism: The Challenge of Abundance," *Reporter*, 14 (May 3, 1956), 8–11.

——. "The Future of Socialism: The Perspective Now," *Partisan Review*, 14 (May-June, 1947), 229–42.

——. "Good Fences Make Good Neighbors," *Fortune*, 34 (August, 1946), 131–35, 161–71.

——. "Guide Posts for Peace," *American Mercury*, 63 (November, 1946), 629–33.

——. "The Highbrow in American Politics," *Partisan Review*, 20 (March-April, 1953), 156–65.

——. "His Eyes Have Seen the Glory," *Collier's*, 119 (February 22, 1947), 12–13, 34–40.

——. "His Rendezvous with Destiny," *New Republic*, 144 (April 15, 1946), 550–54.

——. "The Historian and History," *Foreign Affairs*, 41 (April, 1963), 474–90.

——. "The Historian as Artist," *Atlantic Monthly*, 212 (July, 1963), 35–41.

——. "The History of Business and Vice Versa," *Reporter*, 10 (March 30, 1954), 38–40.

——. "How We Will Vote," *Atlantic Monthly*, 178 (October, 1946), 37–42.

——. "The Humanist Looks at Empirical Social Science," *American Sociological Review*, 27 (December, 1962), 768–71.

——. *Kennedy or Nixon: Does It Make Any Difference?* New York: Macmillan Co., 1960.

——. "The Kremlin's Unruly Little Brothers," *Harper's*, 220 (February, 1960), 67–76.

——. "The Legacy of Andrew Jackson," *American Mercury*, 64 (February, 1947), 168–73.

——. "Liberal Anti-Communism Revisited," *Commentary*, 44 (September, 1967), 68–71.

——. "Liberalism," *Saturday Review*, 40 (June 8, 1957), 11–12, 37.

————. "Liberty and the Liberal," *Commentary*, 14 (July, 1952), 83–84.

————. "The Many Faces of Communism," *Harper's*, 220 (January, 1960), 52–58.

————. "Middle-Aged Man with a Horn," *New Republic*, 128 (March 16, 1953), 16–17.

————. A Middle Way Out of Vietnam," *New York Times Magazine*, September 18, 1966, p. 47.

————. "A Modern Man's Progress," *New Republic*, 129 (November 9, 1953), 16–17.

————. "The Need for an Intelligent Opposition," *New York Times Magazine*, April 2, 1950.

————. "Need Seen for Path Between Moralism and Realism," *Foreign Policy Bulletin*, 30 (February 23, 1951), 1–2.

————. "The New Conservatism: Politics of Conservatism," *Reporter*, 12 (June 16, 1955), 9–12.

————. "The New Conservatism in America: A Liberal Comment," *Confluence*, 2 (December, 1953), 61–71.

————. "The New Isolationism," *Atlantic Monthly*, 189 (May, 1952), 34–38.

————. "On the Inscrutability of History," *Encounter*, 27 (November, 1966), 1–17.

————. "The One Against the Many." In *Paths of American Thought*, ed. Arthur M. Schlesinger, Jr., and Morton White. Boston: Houghton Mifflin Co., 1963.

————. "The Oppenheimer Case," *Atlantic Monthly*, 194 (October, 1954), 29–36.

————. *Orestes A. Brownson: A Pilgrim's Progress*. Boston: Little, Brown and Co., 1939.

————. "Our Country and Our Culture," *Partisan Review*, 19 (September-October, 1952), 590–93.

————. "The Pendulum of Dogma," *Saturday Review*, 37 (April 3, 1954), 15–16, 61.

———— ."The Plight of the American Intellectual," *New Republic*, 134 (June 4, 1956), 19–20.

————. "Political Culture in the United States," *The Nation*, 166 (March 13, 1948), 306–8.

————. *The Politics of Hope*. Boston: Houghton Mifflin Co., 1963.

————. "Probing the American Experience," *New Statesman*, 56 (September 6, 1958), 296, 300, 302.

————. "The Problem of Richard Hildreth," *New England Quarterly*, 13 (June, 1940), 223–45.

————. "Psychological Warfare: Can It Sell Freedom?" *Reporter*, 8 (March 31, 1953), 9–12.

————. Review of *Tomorrow A New World: The New Deal Community Program*, by Paul K. Conklin, *American Historical Review*, 65 (July, 1960), 933–34.

————. "Richard Hofstadter." In *Pastmasters: Some Essays on American Historians*, ed. Marcus Cunliffe and Robin Winks. New York, Evanston, Ill., and London: Harper and Row, 1969.

————. "The Right Man for the Big Job," *New York Times Magazine*, April 3, 1960, p. 120.

————. "The Right to Loathsome Ideas," *Saturday Review*, 32 (May 14, 1949), 17–18, 47.

————. "Roosevelt and His Detractors," *Harper's*, 200 (June, 1950), 62–68.

————. "Sources of the New Deal." In *Paths of American Thought*, ed. Arthur M. Schlesinger, Jr., and Morton White. Boston: Houghton Mifflin Co., 1963.

————. "Stevenson and the American Liberal Dilemma," *Twentieth Century*, 153 (January, 1953), 24–29.

————. "Theology and Politics from the Social Gospel to the Cold War: The Impact of Reinhold Niebuhr." In *Intellectual History in America: From Darwin to Niebuhr*.

Vol. II. Ed. Cushing Strout. New York, Evanston, Ill., and London: Harper and Row, 1968.

———. *A Thousand Days: John F. Kennedy in the White House.* Boston: Houghton Mifflin Co., 1965.

———. "The Thread of History: Freedom or Fatality," *Reporter*, 13 (December 15, 1955), 45–47.

———. *"Time* and the Intellectuals," *New Republic*, 135 (July 16, 1956), 15–17.

———. "The U.S. Communist Party," *Life*, 21 (July 29, 1946), 84–96.

———. *The Vital Center: The Politics of Freedom.* Boston: Houghton Mifflin Co., 1949.

———. "What Eisenhower Was," *The Nation*, 162 (May 25, 1946), 629–30.

———. "What Is Loyalty? A Difficult Question," *New York Times Magazine*, November 2, 1947, p. 7.

———. "What Kind of President Will Johnson Make Now?" *U.S. News and World Report*, 57 (November, 1964), 53–55.

———. "Where Does the Liberal Go from Here?" *New York Times Magazine*, August 4, 1957, p. 7.

———. "Whittaker Chambers and His 'Witness,'" *Saturday Review*, 35 (May 24, 1952), 8–10, 39–40.

———, ed. *The American Revolution: Two Centuries of Interpretation.* Englewood Cliffs, N.J., and New York: Prentice-Hall, 1965.

———, ed. *The Founding of Massachusetts: Historians and the Sources.* Indianapolis, New York, and Kansas City: Bobbs-Merrill Co., 1964.

Schlesinger, Arthur M., Jr.; Coser, Lewis A; Gass, Oscar; and Morgenthau, Hans. "America and the World Revolution," *Commentary*, 36 (October, 1963), 278–96.

Schlesinger, Arthur M., Jr., and White, Morton, eds. *Paths of American Thought.* Boston: Houghton Mifflin Co., 1963.

## SECONDARY SOURCES

*Books*

Aaron, Daniel. *Writers on the Left: Episodes in American Literary Communism.* New York: Harcourt, Brace and World, 1961.

Aron, Raymond. *The Opium of the Intellectuals.* Trans. Terence Kilmartin. Garden City, N.Y.: Doubleday and Co., 1957.

Bachrach, Peter. *The Theory of Democratic Elites: A Critique.* Boston: Little, Brown and Co., 1967.

Bancroft, George. *The History of the United States of America from the Discovery of the Continent.* Abridged and ed. Russel B. Nye. Chicago and London: University of Chicago Press, 1966.

Barr, Stringfellow. *Purely Academic.* New York: Simon and Schuster, 1958.

Beard, Charles A. *The Republic: Conversations on Fundamentals.* New York: Viking Press, 1943.

Beard, Charles A., and Beard, Mary R. *America in Midpassage.* New York: Macmillan Co., 1939.

———. *The American Spirit: A Study of the Idea of Civilization in the United States.* New York: Macmillan Co., 1942.

Becker, Carl L. *The Declaration of Independence: A Study in the History of Political Ideas.* New York: Vintage Books, 1960.

———. *Everyman His Own Historian: Essays on History and Politics.* Chicago: Quadrangle Books, 1966.

———. *The Heavenly City of the Eighteenth Century Philosophers.* New Haven: Yale University Press, 1952.

———. *The History of Political Parties in the Province of New York, 1770–1776.* Madison, Wis.: University of Wisconsin Press, 1909.

――. *Modern Democracy.* New Haven: Yale University Press, 1941.

Bell, Daniel. *The End of Ideology: On the Exhaustion of Political Ideas in the Fifties.* Glencoe, Ill.: Free Press, 1960.

――, ed. *The Radical Right.* Garden City, N.Y.: Anchor Books, 1964.

Benda, Julian. *The Treason of the Intellectuals.* Trans. Richard Aldington. New York: William Morrow and Co., 1928.

Bendix, Richard. *Max Weber: An Intellectual Portrait.* Garden City, N.Y.: Anchor Books, 1962.

Benson, Lee. *The Concept of Jacksonian Democracy: New York as a Test Case.* Princeton: Princeton University Press, 1961.

Berman, Ronald. *America in the Sixties: An Intellectual History.* New York: Free Press, 1968.

Bluhm, William T. *Theories of the Political System: Classics of Political Thought and Modern Political Analysis.* Englewood Cliffs, N.J.: Prentice-Hall, 1965.

Blum, John M., et al. *The National Experience: A History of the United States.* New York: Harcourt, Brace and World, 1968.

Buckley, William F., Jr. *God and Man at Yale: The Superstitions of "Academic Freedom."* Chicago: Henry Regnery Co., 1951.

Bunzel, John H. *Anti-Politics in America: Reflections on the Anti-Political Temper and Its Distortions of the Democratic Process.* New York: Alfred A. Knopf, 1967.

Burns, James McGregor. *Congress on Trial: The Legislative Process and the Administrative State.* New York: Harper and Bros., 1949.

Campbell, Angus, et al. *The American Voter.* New York, London, and Sydney: John Wiley and Sons, 1965.

Chase, Richard. *The Democratic Vista: A Dialogue on Life*

*and Letters in Contemporary America.* Garden City, N.Y.: Doubleday and Co., 1958.

Cohen, Mitchell, and Hale, Dennis, eds. *The New Student Left: An Anthology.* Boston: Beacon Press, 1966.

Commager, Henry Steele. *The American Mind: An Interpretation of American Thought and Character Since the 1880's.* New Haven: Yale University Press, 1957.

Coser, Lewis A. *The Functions of Social Conflict.* Glencoe, Ill.: Free Press, 1956.

Cowley, Malcolm. *Exile's Return: A Narrative of Ideas.* New York: W. W. Norton and Co., 1934.

Crick, Bernard. *The American Science of Politics: Its Origins and Conditions.* Berkeley and Los Angeles: University of California Press, 1959.

———. *In Defense of Politics.* London: Weidenfield and Nicolson, 1962.

Curti, Merle. *American Paradox: The Conflict of Thought and Action.* New Brunswick, N.J.: Rutgers University Press, 1956.

———. *The Growth of American Thought.* New York and London: Harper and Bros., 1943.

Davis, Harry R., and Good, Robert C., eds. *Reinhold Niebuhr on Politics: His Political Philosophy and Its Application to Our Age as Expressed in His Writings.* New York: Charles Scribner's Sons, 1960.

Dewey, John. *The Public and Its Problems.* Denver: Allan Swallow, n.d.

Ekirch, Arthur A., Jr. *Ideologies and Utopias: The Impact of the New Deal on American Thought.* Chicago: Quadrangle Books, 1969.

Evans, Richard E. *Dialogue with Erich Fromm.* New York: Harper and Row, 1966.

Fiedler, Leslie. *An End to Innocence: Essays on Culture and Politics.* Boston: Beacon Press, 1955.

Forcey, Charles. *The Crossroads of Liberalism: Croly, Weyl, Lippmann and the Progressive Era, 1900–1925.* New York: Oxford University Press, 1961.

Freund, Julian. *The Sociology of Max Weber.* Trans. Mary Ilford. New York: Pantheon Books, 1968.

Fromm, Erich. *Beyond the Chains of Illusion: My Encounter with Marx and Freud.* New York: Simon and Schuster, 1962.

——. *Escape from Freedom.* New York and Toronto: Rinehart and Co., 1941.

——. *Man for Himself: An Inquiry into the Psychology of Ethics.* Greenwich, Conn.: Fawcett Publications, 1967.

——. *Psychoanalysis and Religion.* New Haven: Yale University Press, 1950.

——. *The Sane Society.* New York and Toronto: Rinehart and Co., 1955.

Gabriel, Ralph Henry. *The Course of American Democratic Thought: An Intellectual History Since 1815.* New York: Ronald Press Co., 1940.

Gargan, Edward T. *Alexis de Tocqueville: The Critical Years, 1848–1851.* Washington: Catholic University of America Press, 1955.

Gerth, H. H., and Millis, C. Wright, eds. *From Max Weber: Essays in Sociology.* New York: Oxford University Press, 1958.

Gilbert, James Burkhart. *Writers and Partisans: A History of Literary Radicalism in America.* New York: John Wiley and Sons, 1968.

Goldman, Eric F. *Rendezvous with Destiny: A History of Modern American Reform.* New York: Vintage Books, 1958.

——. *The Tragedy of Lyndon Johnson.* New York: Alfred A. Knopf, 1969.

Greene, Jack P. *The Reappraisal of the American Revolution in Recent Historical Literature*. Baltimore: American Historical Association, 1967.

Guinsburg, Thomas N., ed. *The Dimensions of History*. Chicago: Rand McNally and Co., 1971.

Harrington, Michael. *The Other America: Poverty in the United States*. Baltimore: Penguin Books, 1965.

Hart, Jeffrey. *The American Dissent: A Decade of Modern Conservatism*. Garden City, N.Y.: Doubleday and Co., 1966.

Hartshorne, Thomas L. *The Distorted Image: Changing Conceptions of the American Character Since Turner*. Cleveland: The Press of Case Western Reserve University, 1968.

Heimert, Alan E. *Religion and the American Mind, from the Great Awakening to the Revolution*. Cambridge: Harvard University Press, 1966.

Herr, Richard. *Tocqueville and the Old Regime*. Princeton: Princeton University Press, 1962.

Higham, John; Krieger, Leonard; and Gilbert, Felix. *History*. Englewood Cliffs, N.J.: Prentice-Hall, 1965.

Hoffer, Eric. *The True Believer*. New York: Mentor Books, 1958.

Howe, Irving, and Coser, Lewis. *The American Communist Party: A Critical History, 1919–1957*. Boston: Beacon Press, 1957.

Howe, Irving. *Steady Work: Essays in the Politics of Democratic Radicalism, 1953–1966*. New York: Harcourt, Brace and World, 1966.

Hughes, H. Stuart. *Consciousness and Society: The Reorientation of European Social Thought, 1890–1930*. New York: Alfred A. Knopf, 1958.

Huszar, George B., ed. *The Intellectuals: A Controversial Portrait*. Glencoe, Ill.: Free Press, 1960.

James, William A. *A Pluralistic Universe*. New York: Long-mans, Green, and Co., 1909.

———. *Pragmatism: A New Name for Some Old Ways of Thinking*. New York: Longmans, Green, and Co., 1958.

———. *The Varieties of Religious Experience: A Study of Human Nature*. New York: Mentor Books, 1958.

Jameson, J. Franklin. *The American Revolution Considered as a Social Movement*. Princeton: Princeton University Press, 1926.

Kazin, Alfred. *Starting Out in the Thirties*. Boston: Little, Brown and Co., 1965.

Kegley, Charles W., and Bretall, Robert W., eds. *Reinhold Niebuhr: His Religious, Social, and Political Thought*. New York: Macmillan Co., 1956.

Kirk, Russell. *The Conservative Mind from Burke to Santayana*. Chicago: Henry Regnery Co., 1953.

Kolko, Gabriel. *The Triumph of Conservatism: A Reinterpretation of American History, 1900–1916*. Chicago: Quadrangle Books, 1967.

Kornhauser, William. *The Politics of Mass Society*. Glencoe, Ill.: Free Press, 1963.

Lasch, Christopher. *The New Radicalism in America, 1889–1963: The Intellectual as a Social Type*. New York: Alfred A. Knopf, 1965.

Lasswell, Harold D. *Politics: Who Gets What, When, How*. Cleveland and New York: World Publishing Co., 1961.

———. *Power and Personality*. New York: W. W. Norton and Co., 1948.

———. *Psychopathology and Politics*. New York: The Viking Press, 1960.

———. *World Politics and Personal Insecurity*. New York, London: McGraw-Hill Book Co., 1935.

Lasswell, Harold D., and Lerner, Daniel, eds. *World Revolutionary Elites: Studies in Coercive Ideological Move-*

*ments*. Cambridge, Mass.: Massachusetts Institute of Technology Press, 1965.

Lazarsfeld, Paul F., and Thielens, Wagner, Jr. *The Academic Mind: Social Scientists in a Time of Crisis*. Glencoe, Ill.: Free Press, 1958.

Lipset, Seymour Martin. *Political Man: The Social Bases of Politics*. Garden City, N.Y.: Anchor Books, 1963.

Lynd, Staughton. *Intellectual Origins of American Radicalism*. New York: Pantheon Books, 1968.

MacDonald, Malcolm H., ed. *The Intellectual in Politics*. Austin: University of Texas Press, 1966.

Mannheim, Karl. *Essays on Sociology and Social Psychology*, ed. Paul Kecskemiti. New York: Oxford University Press, 1933.

———. *Essays on the Sociology of Knowledge*, ed. Paul Kecskemeti. Oxford University Press, 1952.

———. *Freedom, Power, and Democratic Planning*. New York: Oxford University Press, 1950.

———. *Ideology and Utopia: An Introduction to the Sociology of Knowledge*. Trans. Louis Wirth and Edward Shils. New York: Harcourt, Brace and World, n.d.

May, Henry, ed. *The Discontent of the Intellectuals: A Problem of the Twenties*. Chicago: Rand McNally and Co., 1963.

Mayer, J. P. *Alexis de Tocqueville: A Biographical Essay in Political Science*. Trans. M. M. Boxman and C. Hahn. New York: Viking Press, 1940.

Mead, George H. *Mind, Self, and Society from the Standpoint of a Social Behaviorist*. Chicago: University of Chicago Press, 1934.

Meyers, Marvin. *The Jacksonian Persuasion: Politics and Belief*. Stanford, Calif.: Stanford University Press, 1968.

Milbrath, Lester W. *Political Participation: How and Why*

*Do People Get Involved in Politics?* Chicago: Rand Mc-Nally and Co., 1966.

Mills, C. Wright. *The Sociological Imagination.* New York: Oxford University Press, 1959.

———. *White Collar: The American Middle Classes.* New York: Oxford University Press, 1956.

Minar, David W. *Ideas and Politics: The American Experience.* Homewood, Ill.: The Dorsey Press, 1964.

Molnar, Thomas. *The Decline of the Intellectual.* Cleveland and New York: World Publishing Co., 1965.

Moore, Edward C. *American Pragmatism: Pierce, James, and Dewey.* New York: Columbia University Press, 1961.

Newman, William J. *The Futilitarian Society.* New York: George Braziller, 1961.

Niebuhr, Reinhold. *The Children of Light and the Children of Darkness: A Vindication of Democracy and a Critique of Its Traditional Defense.* New York: Charles Scribner's Sons, 1944.

———. *Christian Realism and Political Problems.* New York: Charles Scribner's Sons, 1953.

———. *The Irony of American History.* New York: Charles Scribner's Sons, 1952.

———. *Pious and Secular America.* New York: Charles Scribner's Sons, 1958.

Nisbet, Robert A. *The Quest for Community: A Study in the Ethics of Order and Freedom.* New York: Oxford University Press, 1953.

Noble, David W. *Historians Against History: The Frontier Thesis and the National Covenant in American Historical Writing Since 1830.* Minneapolis: University of Minnesota Press, 1965.

Parrington, Vernon. *Main Currents in American Thought.* Vol. I. New York: Harcourt, Brace and World, 1954.

Parsons, Talcott. *The Structure of Social Action: A Study of Social Theory with Special Reference to a Group of Recent European Writers.* Glencoe, Ill., and New York: Free Press, 1961.

Pollack, Norman. *The Populist Response to Industrial America.* New York: W. W. Norton Co., 1962.

Riesman, David; Glazer, Nathan; and Denney, Reuel. *The Lonely Crowd: A Study in the Changing American Character.* New Haven: Yale University Press, 1950.

Rockwood, Raymond O. *Carl Becker's Heavenly City Revisited.* Ithaca, N.Y.: Cornell University Press, 1958.

Rogin, Michael Paul. *The Intellectuals and McCarthy: The Radical Spectre.* Cambridge, Mass., and London: Massachusetts Institute of Technology Press, 1967.

Rogow, Arnold, and Lasswell, Harold B. *Power, Corruption, and Rectitude.* Englewood Cliffs, N.J.: Prentice-Hall, 1963.

Rossiter, Clinton. *Conservatism in America.* New York: Alfred A. Knopf, 1956.

Rovere, Richard. *Senator Joe McCarthy.* Cleveland and New York: World Publishing Co., 1965.

Schaar, John H. *Escape from Authority: The Perspectives of Erich Fromm.* New York: Basic Books, 1961.

Schlesinger, Arthur M. *Colonial Merchants and the American Revolution.* New York: Columbia University Studies in History, Economics, and Public Law, 1918.

Simpson, M. C. M., ed. *Correspondence and Conversations of Alexis de Tocqueville with Nassau William Senior from 1834 to 1859.* 2 vols. London: Henry S. King and Co., 1872.

Skolnick, Jerome H. *The Politics of Protest.* New York: Ballantine Books, 1969.

Skotheim, Robert Allen. *American Intellectual Histories and*

*Historians.* Princeton, N.J.: Princeton University Press, 1966.

Snyder, Phil L., ed. *Detachment and the Writing of History: Essays and Letters of Carl L. Becker.* Ithaca, N.Y.: Cornell University Press, 1958.

Stone, I. F. *The Haunted Fifties.* New York: Random House, 1963.

Stouffer, Samuel A. *Communism, Conformity, and Civil Liberties: A Cross-Section of the Nation Speaks Its Mind.* Gloucester, Mass.: Peter Smith, 1963.

Strout, Cushing, ed. *Intellectual History in America: From Darwin to Niebuhr.* 2 vols. New York, Evanston, Ill., and London: Harper and Row, 1968.

———. *The Pragmatic Revolt in American History: Carl Becker and Charles Beard.* New Haven: Yale University Press, 1958.

Tocqueville, Alexis de. *Democracy in America.* Trans. Phillips Bradley. 2 vols. New York: Vintage Books, 1945.

———. *The Old Regime and the French Revolution.* Trans. Stuart Gilbert. Garden City, N.Y.: Doubleday Anchor Books, 1955.

Trilling, Lionel. *The Liberal Imagination: Essays on Literature and Society.* Garden City, N.Y.: Doubleday and Co., 1957.

Viereck, Peter. *Conservatism Revisited: The Revolt Against Revolt, 1815–1949.* New York: Charles Scribner's Sons, 1949.

Warren, Frank A., III. *Liberals and Communism: The "Red Decade" Revisited.* Bloomington, Ind., and London: Indiana University Press, 1966.

Weber, Max. *The Protestant Ethic and the Spirit of Capitalism.* Trans. Talcott Parsons. New York: Charles Scribner's Sons, 1958.

———. *The Sociology of Religion.* Trans. Ephraim Fischoff. Boston: Beacon Press, 1963.

White, Morton G. *Social Thought in America: The Revolt Against Formalism.* New York: Viking Press, 1949.

Wise, Gene. *Explaining Historical Studies: Some Strategies for Inquiry.* Homewood, Ill.: Dorsey Press, forthcoming.

Wish, Harvey. *The American Historian: A Social-Intellectual History of the Writing of the American Past.* New York: Oxford University Press, 1960.

Zetterbaum, Marvin. *Tocqueville and the Problem of Democracy.* Stanford, Calif.: Stanford University Press, 1967.

Zinn, Howard. *The Politics of History.* Boston: Beacon Press, 1970.


*Articles*

Aaron, Daniel. "Conservatism, Old and New," *American Quarterly*, 6 (Summer, 1954), 99–110.

———. Review of *The American Political Tradition*, by Richard Hofstadter, *American Quarterly*, 1 (Spring, 1949), 94–96.

Aiken, Henry David. "The Revolt Against Ideology," *Commentary*, 37 (April, 1964), 29–40.

American Political Science Association. "Towards a More Responsible Two-Party System: A Report of the Committee on Political Parties," Supplement to *American Political Science Review*, 44 (September, 1950).

Bailyn, Bernard. "History and the Distrust of Knowledge," *New Republic*, 139 (December 15, 1958), 17–18.

Barber, Bernard. "Sociological Aspects of Anti-Intellectualism," *Journal of Social Issues*, 11:3 (1955), 25–30.

Barzun, Jacques. "Artist Against Society: Some Articles of War," *Partisan Review*, 19 (January-February, 1952), 60–77.

Becker, Carl L. "What Is Historiography?" *American Historical Review*, 44 (October, 1938), 20–28.

Bell, Daniel. "Interpretations of American Politics." In *The Radical Right*, ed. Daniel Bell. Garden City, N.Y.: Anchor Books, 1964.

Bell, Daniel, and Aiken, Henry David. "Ideology—A Debate," *Commentary*, 38 (October, 1964), 69–76.

Bell, Witfield J. Review of *The Gentle Puritan: The Life of Ezra Stiles, 1727–1795*, by Edmund S. Morgan, *William and Mary Quarterly*, 3rd ser. 21 (January, 1964), 121–23.

Bendix, Reinhard. "The Image of Man in the Social Sciences: The Basic Assumptions of Present-Day Research," *Commentary*, 11 (February, 1951), 187–92.

Bestor, Arthur. *Review of Anti-Intellectualism in American Life*, by Richard Hofstadter, *American Historical Review*, 70 (July, 1965), 1118–20.

Brademas, John. "The Role of the Intellectual in Politics—An American View." In *The Intellectual in Politics*, ed. Malcolm H. MacDonald. Austin: University of Texas Press, 1966.

Brown, Stuart M., Jr. "The Theology of Reinhold Niebuhr," *Review of Religion*, 12 (March, 1948), 262–76.

Burks, Richard V. "A Conception of Ideology for Historians," *Journal of the History of Ideas*, 10 (April, 1949), 183–98.

Champney, Freeman. "The White Collar Man's Burden," *Antioch Review*, 1 (December, 1941), 463–73.

Chartier, Barbara. "The Social Role of the Literary Elite," *Social Forces*, 29 (December, 1950), 179–86.

Christian, William A. "Belief, Inquiry, and the 'Dilemma' of the Liberal," *The Journal of Religion*, 31 (April, 1951), 79–90.

Clark, John Abbot, "What Is an Intellectual?" *South Atlantic Quarterly*, 40 (July, 1941), 228–35.

Cogley, John. "The Bouncing Ball," *Commonweal*, 66 (August 23, 1957), 522.

Commager, Henry Steele. "Should Historians Write Contemporary History?" *Saturday Review*, 49 (February 12, 1966), 18–20, 47.

Coombs, Robert H. "Karl Mannheim, Epistemology and the Sociology of Knowledge," *Sociological Quarterly*, 7 (Spring, 1966), 229–33.

Coser, Lewis A. "Intellectuals and Men of Power—Two Case Histories." In *The Intellectuals: A Controversial Portrait*, ed. George B. Huszar. Glencoe, Ill.: Free Press, 1960.

Cronin, Morton. "The American Intellectual," *American Association of University Professors Bulletin*, 14 (Summer, 1958), 403–14.

Crick, Bernard. "The Strange Quest for an American Conservatism," *The Review of Politics*, 17 (July, 1953), 359–76.

Cunliffe, Marcus. "Arthur M. Schlesinger, Jr." In *Pastmasters: Some Essays on American Historians*, ed. Marcus Cunliffe and Robin W. Winks. New York, Evanston, Ill., and London: Harper and Row, 1969.

Curti, Merle. "The Democratic Theme in American Historical Literature," *Journal of American History*, 39 (June, 1952), 23–28.

———. "The Great Mr. Locke, America's Philosopher, 1783–1861," *Huntington Library Bulletin*, 11 (April, 1937), 107–51.

———. "Intellectuals and Other People," *American Historical Review*, 60 (January, 1955), 259–82.

*Daedalus*, 88. "Comments on Lipset's 'American Intellectuals: Their Politics and Status'" (Summer, 1959), 487–98.

Dahrendorf, Ralf. "Out of Utopia: Toward a Reorientation of Sociological Theory." In *Sociological Theory: A Book of Readings*, ed. Lewis A. Coser and Bernard Rosenberg. New York: Macmillan Co., 1964.

Davis, Lane. "The Cost of Realism: Contemporary Restatements of Democracy," *Western Political Quarterly*, 17 (March, 1964), 37–46.

Diggins, John P. "Consciousness and Ideology in American History: The Burden of Daniel J. Boorstin," American Historical Review, 76 (February, 1971), 99–118.

———. "The Perils of Naturalism: Some Reflections on Daniel J. Boorstin's Approach to American History," *American Quarterly*, 23 (May, 1971), 153–80.

Duncan, Graeme, and Lukes, Steven. "The New Democracy," *Political Studies*, 11 (June, 1963), 156–77.

Eby, Kermit. "Politics for the Intellectual," *Antioch Review*, 4 (September, 1944), 327–37.

Eisenstadt, A. S. "The Perennial Myth—Writing American History Today," *Massachusetts Review*, 7 (Autumn, 1966), 757–79.

Elliot, Robert C. "The Fear of Utopia," *Centennial Review*, 7 (Spring, 1963), 237–51.

Etzioni, Amitai. "Neo-Liberalism—The Turn of the 60's," *Commentary*, 30 (December, 1960), 473–79.

Fairlie, Henry. "Johnson and the Intellectuals," *Commentary*, 40 (October, 1965), 49–55.

Fischer, David Hackett. "John Beale Bordley, Daniel Boorstin, and the American Enlightenment," *Journal of Southern History*, 28 (August, 1962), 327–42.

Fitch, Robert E. "The Illusions of the Intelligentsia," *Commentary*, 16 (December, 1953), 562–67.

———. "Reinhold Niebuhr as Prophet and as Philosopher of History," *Journal of Religion*, 32 (January, 1952), 31–46.

———. "Reinhold Niebuhr, Excubitor," *Pacific Spectator*, 4 (Summer, 1950), 306–18.

Flinn, Thomas A., and Wirt, Frederick M. "Local Party Leaders: Groups of Like Minded Men." In *Political Behavior in America: New Directions*, ed. Heinz Eulau. New York: Random House, 1966.

Frisch, Morton J. "Roosevelt the Conservator: A Rejoinder to Hofstadter," *Journal of Politics*, 25 (May, 1963), 361–72.

Gabriel, Ralph Henry. Review of *The Liberal Tradition in America*, by Louis Hartz, *Journal of the History of Ideas*, 17 (January, 1956), 136–68.

Genovese, Eugene B. "Marxian Interpretations of the Slave South." In *Towards a New Past: Dissenting Essays in American History*, ed. Barton J. Bernstein. New York: Pantheon Books, 1968.

Gold, Milton. "In Search of a Historian," *Centennial Review*, 7 (Summer, 1963), 282–305.

Good, Robert C. "The National Interest and Political Realism: Niebuhr's 'Debate' with Morgenthau and Kennan," *Journal of Politics*, 22 (November, 1960), 597–619.

Greene, Jack P. "The Flight from Determinism: A Review of Recent Literature on the Coming of the American Revolution," *South Atlantic Quarterly*, 61 (1962), 235–59.

Harrington, Michael. "The New Radicalism," *Partisan Review*, 32 (Spring, 1965), 194–205.

Hartung, Frank E. "Problems of the Sociology of Knowledge," *Philosophy of Science*, 19 (January, 1952), 17–32.

Herberg, Will. "The Great Debate," *Commonweal*, 62 (September 5, 1955), 559–62.

Hicks, Granville. "Liberalism in the Fifties," *American Scholar*, 25 (Summer, 1956), 283–96.

Higham, John. "American Intellectual History: A Critical Appraisal." In *The Craft of American History*. Vol. I. Ed. A. S. Eisenstadt. New York: Harper and Row, 1966.

————. "Beyond Consensus: The Historian as Moral Critic," *American Historical Review*, 67 (April, 1962), 609–25.

————. "The Construction of American History." In *The Reconstruction of American History*, ed. John Higham. New York: Harper and Row, 1965.

————. "The Cult of the 'American Consensus': Homogenizing American History," *Commentary*, 27 (February, 1959), 93–100.

————. "Intellectual History and Its Neighbors," *Journal of the History of Ideas*, 15 (June, 1954), 339–47.

————. Review of *The Lost World of Thomas Jefferson*, by Daniel Boorstin, *Journal of American History*, 36 (June, 1949), 133–35.

————. "The Rise of American Intellectual History," *American Historical Review*, 56 (April, 1951), 453–71.

Hollingsworth, J. Rogers. "American Anti-Intellectualism," *South Atlantic Quarterly*, 63 (Summer, 1964), 277–84.

————. "Consensus and Continuity in Recent American Historical Writing," *South Atlantic Quarterly*, 61 (Winter, 1962), 40–50.

Hook, Sidney. "Communism and the Intellectual." In *The Intellectuals: A Controversial Portrait*, ed. George B. Huszar. Glencoe, Ill.: Free Press, 1960.

————. "From Alienation to Critical Integrity: The Vocation of the American Intellectuals." In *The Intellectuals: A Controversial Portrait*, ed. George B. Huszar. Glencoe, Ill.: Free Press, 1960.

Hoover, Dwight W. "Some Comments on Recent United States Historiography," *American Quarterly*, 17 (1965), 299–318.

Howe, Irving. "The Lost Young Intellectual: A Marginal Man, Twice Alienated," *Commentary*, 12 (October, 1946), 361–76.

Hughes, H. Stuart. "Is the Intellectual Obsolete? The Truly Speculating Mind in America," *Commentary*, 22 (October, 1956), 313–19.

Huntington, Samuel P. "Conservatism as an Ideology," *American Political Science Review*, 51 (June, 1957), 454–73.

Jaffa, Harry V. "Conflicts Within the Idea of a Liberal Tradition," *Comparative Studies in Society and History*, 5 (April, 1963), 274–78.

Kariel, Henry S. "The Normative Pattern of Erich Fromm's 'Escape from Freedom,'" *Journal of Politics*, 19 (November, 1957), 640–59.

Kazin, Alfred. "The President and Other Intellectuals," *American Scholar*, 30 (Autumn, 1961), 498–516.

Keniston, Kenneth. "Alienation and the Decline of Utopia," *American Scholar*, 29 (Spring, 1960), 161–200.

Kenyon, Cecilia. Review of *The Americans: The Colonial Experience*, by Daniel Boorstin, *William and Mary Quarterly*, 16 (October, 1959), 585–89.

Kirk, Russell. "The American Intellectual: A Conservative View." In *The Intellectuals: A Controversial Portrait*, ed. George B. Huszar. Glencoe, Ill.: Free Press, 1960.

Kirkendall, Richard S. "Franklin D. Roosevelt and the Service Intellectual," *Journal of American History*, 49 (December, 1962), 456–71.

Kirkland, Edward C. Review of *The Age of Reform from Bryan to F.D.R.*, by Richard Hofstadter, *American Historical Review*, 61 (April, 1956), 666–68.

Koch, Adrienne. "Pragmatic Wisdom and the American Enlightenment," *William and Mary Quarterly*, 3rd ser. 18 (July, 1961), 313–29.

———. Review of *The Liberal Tradition in America*, by Louis Hartz, *Journal of American History*, 42 (December, 1955), 550–52.

Kolko, Gabriel. "A Critique of Max Weber's Philosophy of History," *Ethics*, 70 (October, 1959), 21–36.

Kristol, Irving. "The Idea of Democracy." Paper presented at the 62nd annual meeting of the Organization of American Historians. Philadelphia, Penna., April 18, 1969.

Lasch, Christopher. "The Cultural Cold War: A Short History of the Congress for Cultural Freedom." In *Towards a New American Past: Dissenting Essays in American History*, ed. Barton J. Bernstein. New York: Pantheon Books, 1968.

Lasswell, Harold. "The Psychology of Hitlerism," *Political Quarterly*, 4 (Number 3), 373–84.

Lemisch, Jesse. "The American Revolution Seen from the Bottom Up." In *Towards a New Past: Dissenting Essays in American History*, ed. Barton J. Bernstein. New York: Pantheon Books, 1968.

———. "The Idea of Democracy." Paper presented at the 62nd annual meeting of the Organization of American Historians. Philadelphia, Penna., April 18, 1969.

Leuchtenberg, William E. "Anti-Intellectualism: An Historical Perspective," *Journal of Social Issues*, 11:3 (1955), 8–17.

———. Review of *A Thousand Days*, by Arthur M. Schlesinger, Jr., *American Historical Review*, 72 (October, 1966), 339–40.

Levenstein, Aaron. "The Demagogues and the Intellectual," *Antioch Review*, 13 (September, 1953), 259–74.

Lewis, Gordon K. "The Metaphysics of Conservatism," *Western Political Quarterly*, 6 (December, 1953), 728–41.

Lewis, John D. Review of *The Liberal Tradition in America*, by Louis Hartz, *American Political Science Review*, 49 (December, 1955), 1155–57.

Lichtheim, George. "The Role of the Intellectuals," *Commentary*, 29 (April, 1960), 295–307.

Lipset, Seymour M. "American Intellectuals: Their Politics and Status," *Daedalus*, 88 (Summer, 1959), 460–86.

———. "The Sources of the 'Radical Right.'" In *The Radical Right*, ed. Daniel Bell. Garden City, N.Y.: Anchor Books, 1964.

Loewenberg, Bert James. Review of *Social Darwinism in American Thought*, 1860–1915, by Richard Hofstadter, *American Historical Review*, 50 (July, 1945), 820–21.

Lynd, Helen M. "Realism and the American Intellectual in a Time of Crisis," *American Scholar*, 20 (Winter, 1951–52), 21–32.

Lynd, Staughton. "Beyond Beard." In *Towards a New Past: Dissenting Essays in American History*, ed. Barton J. Bernstein. New York: Pantheon Books, 1968.

———. "Historical Past and Existential Present." In *The Dimensions of History*, ed. Thomas N. Guinsberg. Chicago: Rand McNally and Co., 1971.

MacDonald, Malcolm H. "Some Reflections on Intellectuals." In *The Intellectual in Politics*, ed. Malcolm H. MacDonald. Austin: University of Texas Press, 1966.

MacLeish, Archibald. "The Irresponsibles." In *The Intellectuals: A Controversial Portrait*, ed. George B. Huszar. Glencoe, Ill.: Free Press, 1960.

———. "Loyalty and Freedom," *American Scholar*, 22 (Autumn, 1953), 393–98.

Mann, Arthur. Review of *The Liberal Tradition in America*, by Louis Hartz, *William and Mary Quarterly*, 3rd ser. 12 (October, 1955), 653–55.

Mannheim, Karl. "The Crisis of Culture in the Era of Mass Democracies and Autarchies," *The Sociological Review*, 26 (April, 1934), 105–29.

Mark, Max. "What Image of Man for Political Science," *Western Political Quarterly*, 15 (December, 1962), 593–604.

Marshall, Lynn L., and Drescher, Seymour. "American Historians and Tocqueville's Democracy," *Journal of American History*, 55 (December, 1968), 512–32.

May, Henry P. "The End of American Radicalism," *American Quarterly*, 2 (Winter, 1950), 291–302.

May, Rollo. "A Psychological Approach to Anti-Intellectualism," *Journal of Social Issues*, 11:3 (1955), 41–47.

McCloskey, Herbert. "Consensus and Ideology in American Politics," *American Political Science Review*, 58 (June, 1964), 361–82.

McKitrick, Eric L. " 'Conservatism' Today," *American Scholar*, 27 (Winter, 1957–58), 49–59.

———. "Is There an American Political Philosophy?" *New Republic*, 132 (April 11, 1955), 22–25.

McNaught, Kenneth. "American Progressives and the Great Society," *Journal of American History*, 53 (December, 1966), 504–20.

McPherson, James M. "The Anti-Slavery Legacy." In *Towards a New Past: Dissenting Essays in American History*, ed. Barton J. Bernstein. New York: Pantheon Books, 1968.

McWilliams, Carey. "Foreword." In *The New Student Left: An Anthology*, ed. Mitchell Cohen and Dennis Hale. Boston: Beacon Press, 1966.

———. "Official Policy and Anti-Intellectualism," *Journal of Social Issues*, 11:3 (1955), 18–21.

———. "Reinhold Niebuhr: New Orthodoxy for Old Liberalism," *American Political Science Review*, 56 (December, 1962), 874–85.

Mead, Margaret. "The New Isolationism," *American Scholar*, 24 (Summer, 1955), 378–82.

Merton, Robert. "Karl Mannheim and the Sociology of Knowledge." In *Social Theory and Social Structure*, by Robert Merton. Glencoe, Ill.: Free Press, 1966.

———. "The Role of the Intellectual in Public Bureaucracy," *Social Forces*, 23 (May, 1945), 405–12.

Metzger, Walter P. "Ideology and the Intellectual: A Study of Thorstein Veblen," *Philosophy of Science*, 16 (April, 1949), 125–33.

Meyers, Marvin. "Louis Hartz, The Liberal Tradition in America: An Appraisal," *Comparative Studies in Society and History*, 5 (April, 1963), 261–68.

Miller, Perry. "The Plight of the Lone Wolf," *American Scholar*, 25 (Autumn, 1956), 445–51.

Miller, William Lee. "The Rise of Neo-Orthodoxy." In *Paths of American Thought*, ed. Arthur M. Schlesinger, Jr., and Morton White. Boston: Houghton Mifflin Co., 1963.

Milton, George F. "A Straight Look at Old Hickory," *Saturday Review*, 28 (September 29, 1945), 10–11.

Morgenthau, Hans. "Failure and Challenge," *The New Leader*, 44 (July 3 and 10, 1961), 3–5.

Morison, Samuel Eliot. "Faith of an Historian," *American Historical Review*, 56 (January, 1951), 261–75.

Niebuhr, Reinhold. "The Cause and Cure of American Psychosis," *American Scholar*, 25 (Winter, 1955–56), 11–20.

———. "The Germans: Unhappy Philosophers in Politics," *American Scholar*, 2 (October, 1933), 409–19.

———. "Liberals and the Marxist Heresy." In *The Intellectuals: A Controversial Portrait*, ed. George B. Huszar. Glencoe, Ill.: Free Press, 1960.

———. "Marxism in Eclipse," *The Spectator*, 170 (June 4, 1943), 518–19.

———. "Pacifism Against the Wall," *American Scholar*, 2 (Spring, 1936), 133–41.

———. "Ten Years That Shook My World." In *Power and Civilization: Political Thought in the Twentieth Century*, ed. David Cooperman and E. V. Walter. New York: Thomas Y. Crowell Co.. 1962.

Nisbet, Robert. "What Is an Intellectual?" *Commentary*, 40 (December, 1965), 93–101.

Nixon, H. C. Review of *The Genius of American Politics*, by

Daniel Boorstin, *Journal of American History*, 40 (December, 1953), 570–72.

Noggle, Burl. "Variety and Ambiguity: The Recent Approach to Southern History," *Mississippi Quarterly*, 17 (Winter, 1963–64), 21–35.

Nye, Russell B. Review of *The Lost World of Thomas Jefferson*, by Daniel Boorstin, *American Historical Review*, 55 (January, 1950), 375–77.

Orwell, George. "Writers and Leviathan." In *The Intellectuals: A Controversial Portrait*, ed. George B. Huszar. Glencoe, Ill.: Free Press, 1960.

Parsons, Talcott. "Social Strains in America." In *The Radical Right*, ed. Daniel Bell. Garden City, N.Y.: Anchor Books, 1964.

*Partisan Review*, 19. "Our Country and Culture (May-June, 1952), 282–327; (July-August, 1952), 420–50; (September-October, 1952), 562–97.

Persons, Stow. Review of *The Lost World of Thomas Jefferson*, by Daniel Boorstin, *William and Mary Quarterly*, 3rd ser. 6 (April, 1949), 319–21.

Peterson, Merrill. Review of *The Lost World of Thomas Jefferson*, by Daniel Boorstin, *New England Quarterly*, 22 (September, 1949), 545–48.

Pole, J. R. "The American Past: Is It Still Usable?" *Journal of American Studies*, 1 (April, 1967), 63–78.

Pollack, Norman. "Fear of Man: Populism, Authoritarianism, and the Historian," *Agricultural History*, 39 (April, 1965), 59–76.

———. "Hofstadter on Populism: A Critique of *The Age of Reform*," *Journal of Southern History*, 26 (November, 1960), 478–500.

Prothro, James W., and Grigg, Charles M. "Fundamental Principles of Democracy: Bases of Agreement and Disagreement," *Journal of Politics*, 22 (Spring, 1960), 276–94.

Record, Wilson. "Intellectuals in Social and Racial Movements," *Phylon*, 195 (Third Quarter, 1954), 231–42.

Reston, James. "What Was Killed Was Not Only the President but the Promise." In *American Politics Since 1945*, ed. Richard Dalfiume. Chicago: Quadrangle Books, 1969.

Rexroth, Kenneth. "I'll Sit This One Out," *The Nation*, 191 (September 24, 1960), 172–76.

Rhoades, Dan. "The Prophetic Insight and Theoretical-Analytical Inadequacy of Christian 'Realism,'" *Ethics*, 7 (October, 1964), 1–15.

Rieff, Philip. "History, Psychoanalysis, and the Social Sciences," *Ethics*, 53 (January, 1953), 107–20.

———. "The Origins of Freud's Political Psychology," *Journal of the History of Ideas*, 17 (April, 1956), 235–49.

———. "Psychology and Politics: The Freudian Connection," *World Politics*, 7 (January, 1955), 293–305.

Riesman, David. "Some Observations on Intellectual Freedom," *American Scholar*, 23 (Winter, 1953–54), 9–25.

———. "The Spread of 'Collegiate' Values." In *The Intellectuals: A Controversial Portrait*, ed. George B. Huszar. Glencoe, Ill.: Free Press, 1960.

Rosenberg, Harold. "America's Post-Radical Critics." In *The Intellectuals: A Controversial Portrait*, ed. George B. Huszar. Glencoe, Ill.: Free Press, 1960.

———. "The Herd of Independent Minds: Has the Avant-Garde Its Own Mass Culture?" *Commentary*, 6 (September, 1948), 244–52.

Ross, E. S. "The Post-War Intellectual Climate," *American Sociological Review*, 10 (October, 1945), 648–50.

Rossiter, Clinton. "Roger Williams on the Anvil of Experience," *American Quarterly*, 3 (Spring, 1951), 14–21.

Roucek, Joseph S. "A History of the Concept of Ideology," *Journal of the History of Ideas*, 5 (October, 1944), 479–88.

Rousseas, Stephen. "The New Radicalism," *Partisan Review*, 32 (Summer, 1965), 346–57.

Rousseas, Stephen, and Farganis, James. "The Retreat of the Idealists," *The Nation*, 196 (March 23, 1963), 240–44.

Rovere, Richard. "Letter from Washington," *New Yorker*, 36 (February 4, 1961), 106–12.

Salomon, Albert. "Karl Mannheim, 1893–1947," *Social Research*, 14 (September, 1947), 350–65.

———. "Max Weber's Political Ideas," *Social Research*, 2 (August, 1935), 368–84.

———. "Max Weber's Sociology," *Social Research*, 2 (February, 1935), 60–73.

———. "Tocqueville, Moralist and Sociologist," *Social Research*, 2 (November, 1935), 405–27.

———. "Tocqueville, 1959," *Social Research*, 26 (January, 1959), 449–70.

Sargent, S. Stanfeld. "Introduction to Anti-Intellectualism in the United States," *Journal of Social Issues*, 11:3 (1955), 3–7.

Savelle, Max. Review of *The Birth of the Republic, 1763–1789*, by Edmund S. Morgan, *William and Mary Quarterly*, 3rd ser. 14 (October, 1957), 608–18.

Schneider, Eugene V. "American Liberal-Intellectual Attitudes Toward the Soviet Union," *Social Forces*, 27 (March, 1949), 251–56.

Schumpeter, Joseph A. "The Sociology of the Intellectuals." In *The Intellectuals: A Controversial Portrait*, ed. George B. Huszar. Glencoe, Ill.: Free Press, 1960.

Schwarz, Delmore. "Our Country and Culture," *Partisan Review*, 19 (May-June, 1952), 595–96.

Scott, Andrew M. "The Progressive Era in Perspective," *Journal of Politics*, 21 (November, 1959), 685–701.

Sellers, Charles Grier. "Andrew Jackson Versus the Historians," *Journal of American History*, 44 (March, 1958), 615–34.

Shannon, William V. "The Controversial Historian of the Age of Kennedy," *New York Times Magazine*, November 21, 1965.

Shils, Edward. "Charisma, Order, and Status," *American Sociological Review*, 30 (April, 1965), 199–213.

———. "Daydreams and Nightmares: Reflections on the Criticism of Mass Culture," *Sewanee Review*, 65 (October-December, 1957), 587–608.

———. "Ideology and Civility: On the Politics of the Intellectual," *Sewanee Review*, 66 (July-September, 1958), 450–80.

Smith, Page. "David Ramsey and the Causes of the American Revolution," *William and Mary Quarterly*, 3rd ser. 17 (January, 1960), 51–76.

———. Review of *The Americans: The Colonial Experience*, by Daniel Boorstin, *New England Quarterly*, 32 (June, 1959), 253–255.

Speier, Hans. "Karl Mannheim's Ideology and Utopia." In *Social Order and the Risks of War: Papers in Political Sociology*. New York: George W. Stewart, 1952.

———. "The Social Determination of Knowledge," *Social Research*, 4 (May, 1938), 182–205.

Strout, Cushing. "Tocqueville's Duality: Describing America and Thinking of Europe," *American Quarterly*, 21 (Spring, 1969), 87–99.

Susman, Warren I. "History and the American Intellectual: Uses of a Usable Past," *American Quarterly*, 16 (Summer, 1964), 243–63.

Tager, Jack. "Progressives, Conservatives, and Status Revolution," *Mid-America*, 48 (July, 1966), 162–75.

Tate, Allen. "To Whom Is the Poet Responsible?" In *The In-*

*tellectuals: A Controversial Portrait*, ed. George B. Huszar. Glencoe, Ill.: Free Press, 1960.

Unger, Irwin. "The 'New Left' and American History: Some Recent Trends in United States Historiography," *American Historical Review*, 72 (July, 1967), 1237–63.

Verba, Sidney. "Organization Membership and Democratic Consensus." In *Political Behavior in America: New Directions*, ed. Heinz Eulau. New York: Random House, 1966.

Viereck, Peter. "Liberals and Conservatives, 1789–1951," *Antioch Review*, 11 (December, 1951), 387–96.

Warshow, Robert. "The Legacy of the '30's: Middle Class Mass Culture and the Intellectual's Problem," *Commentary*, 4 (December, 1947), 538–45.

Weber, Max, "Politics as a Vocation." In *From Max Weber: Essays in Sociology*, ed. H. H. Gerth and C. Wright Mills. New York: Oxford University Press, 1958.

———. "Protestant Sects and the Spirit of Capitalism." In *From Max Weber: Essays in Sociology*.

———. "Religious Rejections of the World and Their Direction." In *From Max Weber: Essays in Sociology*.

Welter, Rush. "The History of Ideas in America: An Essay in Redefinition," *Journal of American History*, 51 (March, 1965), 599–614.

White, Morton. "Prologue: Coherence and Correspondence in American Thought." In *Paths of American Thought*, ed. Arthur M. Schlesinger, Jr., and Morton White. Boston: Houghton Mifflin Co., 1963.

Wiebe, Robert. "The Confinements of Consensus," *Triquarterly*, No. 6, 155–58.

Williams, William A. "Schlesinger: Right Crisis—Wrong Order," *The Nation*, 184 (September 10, 1957), 257–60.

Wilson, Francis G. "Public Opinion and the Intellectuals," *American Political Science Review*, 48 (June, 1954), 321–39.

———. "A Theory of Conservatism," *American Political Science Review*, 35 (February, 1941), 29–43.

Wilson, R. J. "United States: The Reassessment of Liberalism," *Journal of Contemporary History*, 2 (January, 1967), 93–105.

Wise, Gene. "Perry Miller's New England Mind," *Journal of the History of Ideas*, 29 (October-December, 1968), 579–600.

Wolpert, J. F. "Notes on the American Intelligentsia," *Partisan Review*, 14 (September-October, 1947), 472–85.

Woodward, C. Vann. "The North and the South of It," *American Scholar*, 35 (Autumn, 1966), 647–58.

———. Review of *The American Political Tradition and the Men Who Made It*, by Richard Hofstadter, *Journal of American History*, 35 (March, 1949), 681–82.

———. "The Southern Ethic in a Puritan World," *William and Mary Quarterly*, 3rd. ser. 25 (July, 1968), 343–70.

Wrong, Dennis. "Reflections on the End of Ideology," *Dissent*, 7 (Summer, 1960), 286–92.

Zorn, Roman J. Review of *The Age of Jackson*, by Arthur M. Schlesinger, Jr., *Journal of American History*, 32 (March, 1946), 590–92.

# INDEX

This book was set in eleven-point Caledonia and printed by
Oberlin Printing Company, Oberlin, Ohio.
It was bound by John H. Dekker & Sons, Inc., Grand Rapids, Michigan.
This book was designed by LaWanda J. McDuffie.

973.072
M846t

**Morton, Marian J**       1937-
    The terrors of ideological politics; liberal historians in a conservative mood ₍by₎ Marian J. Morton.    Cleveland, Press of Case Western Reserve University, 1972.

xi, 192 p.   21 cm.   $5.95

Bibliography: p. 147-185.

1. United States—Historiography.  2. Historians, American.   I. Title.

35789

E175.M6                973'.07'2         78-183309
ISBN 0-8295-0229-7                          MARC

Library of Congress            72